RAKU *GLASS*

by
Boyce Lundstrom

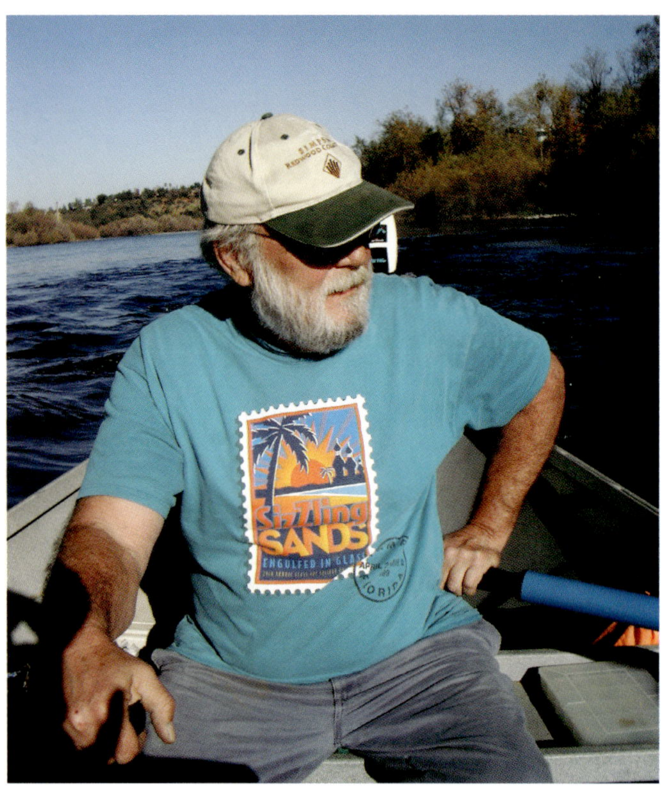

Dedicated to Clif Sowder, my old roomate from school and my first Raku comrade. Still doing glass in Redding, California.

RAKU *GLASS*
A Kiln Firing Process Book One
by Boyce Lundstrom

Book designed by Jorge Atempa

Library of Congress Catalog Card
Number: 2011901041

ISBN Number 978-09825847-1-2

Front Cover:
Tropical Leaves 12”x12” tile
By Boyce Lundstrom

Contents

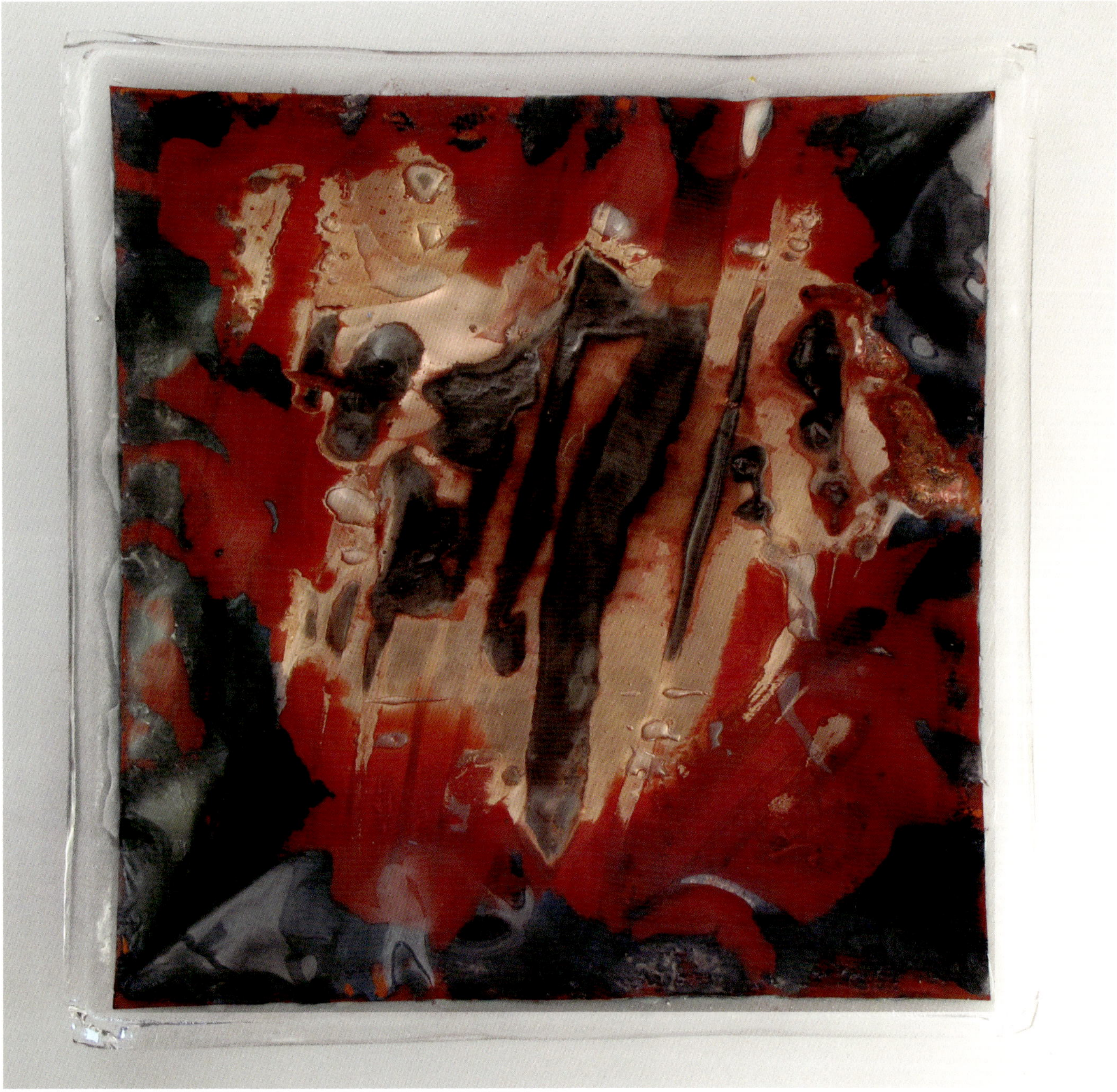

1. *This 8" X 8" dish was done all the way in one play. Painted copper between two blanks of glass, fused and slumped at the same time.*

2. *Close-up of corner showing both pieces of glass.*

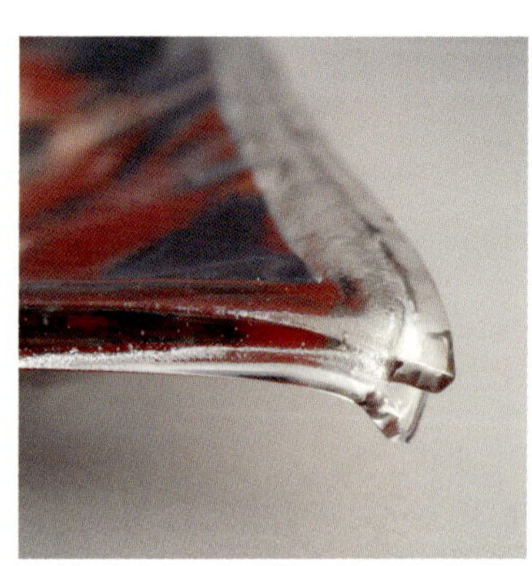

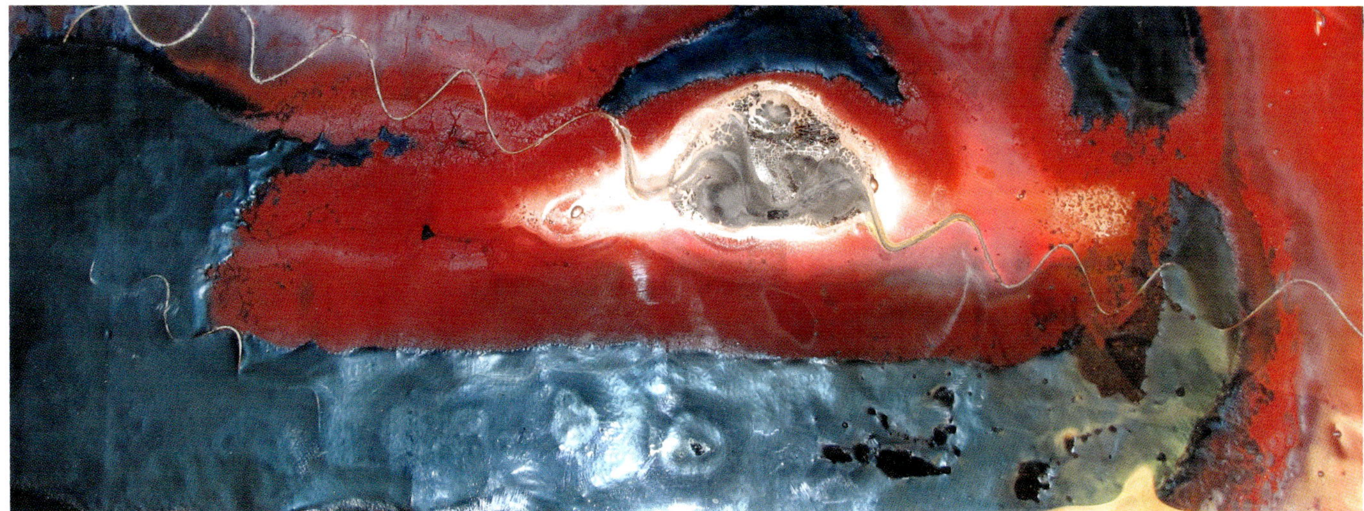

3. *Experiment with Flo Temp, a lead–free instant plumbing solder from TruValue Hardware. Zig-zag copper wire across sushi dish blank with a finger smear of plumbing solder.*

Raku Glass

There is freshness of spirit and attitude when treating glass fusing like the American Raku clay process. Splashing on a glaze or leaving large brush marks is a hallmark of Raku. The shortness of time between executing the concept and the completion of the art piece keeps the process spontaneous and direct, a modern Raku attitude.

Having always wanted to know how things work, I've delved into the chemistry and physics of the glass fusing process. After working with copper inclusions for a few months I experimented with household chemicals to add color and texture resulting in a bit of a change to my attitude and direction. I abandoned the how and why of chemistry and, with growing excitement, simply observed the reactions caused by the heat and atmosphere in the kiln, not knowing what to expect. This, I think, was to explore a kind of modern alchemy. In the spirit of Raku, I now seek surprise and change and a degree of spontaneity as I work with inclusions in fused glass.

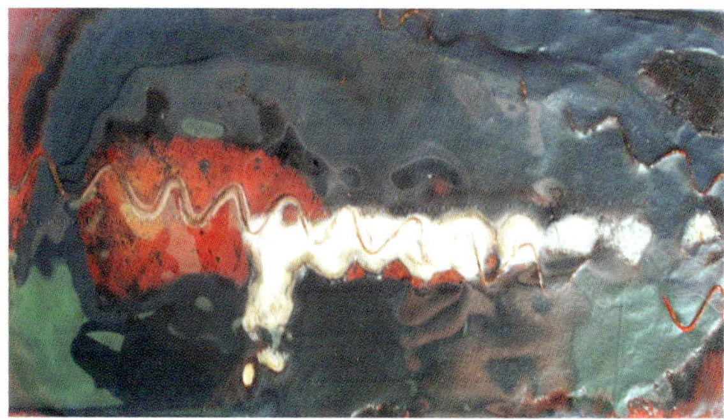

4. *Early experimental tile with wavy bent copper to create channel for escaping gas caused by the copper solder flux as it off-gassed.*

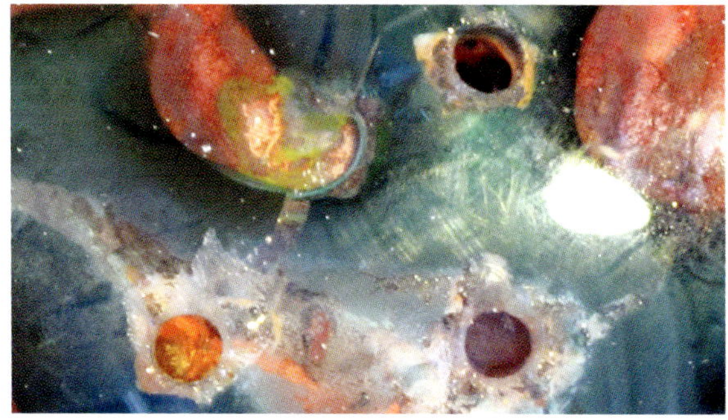

5. *Bubbles – good looking once you expect it. Why not, even big ones? They are usually structurally sound.*

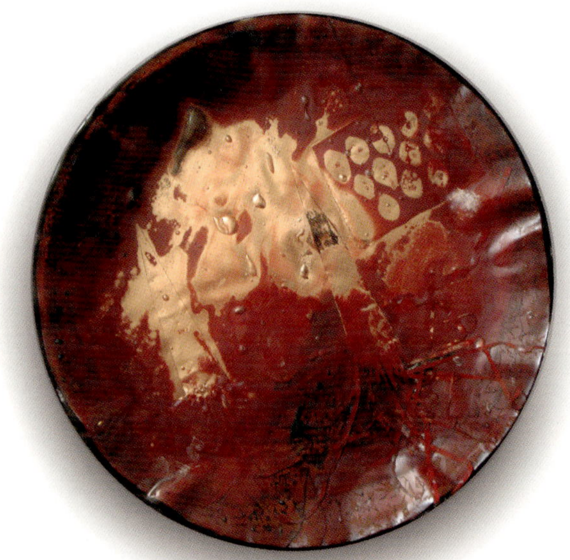

6. *12" plate using boric acid to keep the copper bright and iron granules collected from beach sand to make black shading.*

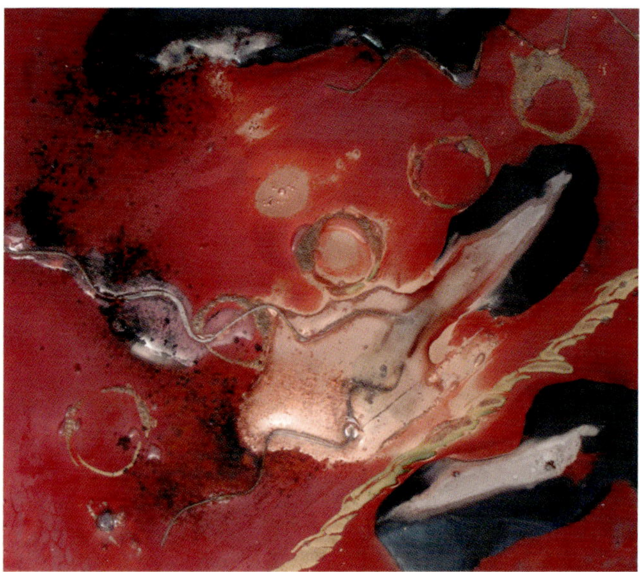

7. *9" X 9" square. White from liquid solder, black from trapped iridescent smoke. The bubbles are fairly large, but after accepting them as part of the piece, you no longer see them as impeding function.*

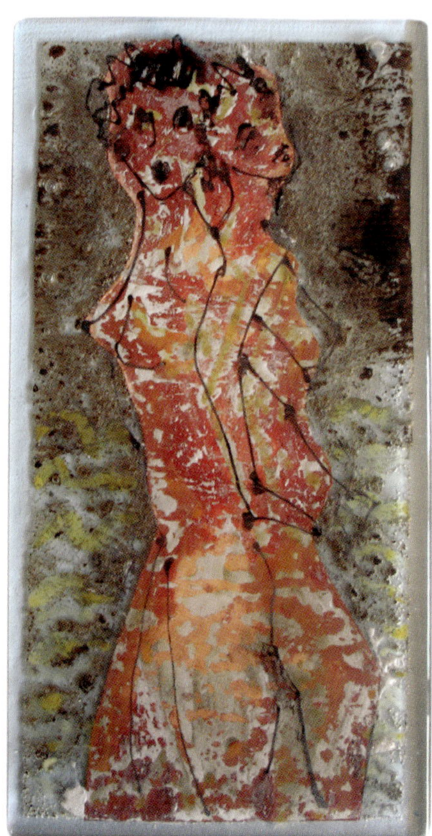

8. *Raku Nudes – copper under aluminum foil. Lines drawn with black Glassline. "Raku" is not always abstract.*

As in Raku, the fire in the kiln alters the copper and produces fuming metals with iridescent qualities, a natural consequence of a reducing atmosphere at high temperatures. I hope to capture the spirit of the performance and then let go and move on. Yahoo Raku.

Raku Rhythm

Rhythm and timing are essential in developing your Raku style and technique when using reactive materials. In the process of painting with alkaline earth on a glass blank, then adding copper to the wet earth coat, the chemical and pyrogenic reactions are sensitive to time and surface contact. The sense of rhythm comes from practice and a thorough knowledge of a process. The process of learning creates confidence, which shows in your work.

In Raku, one generally applies glaze to the pot with a large Japanese brush, rarely covering

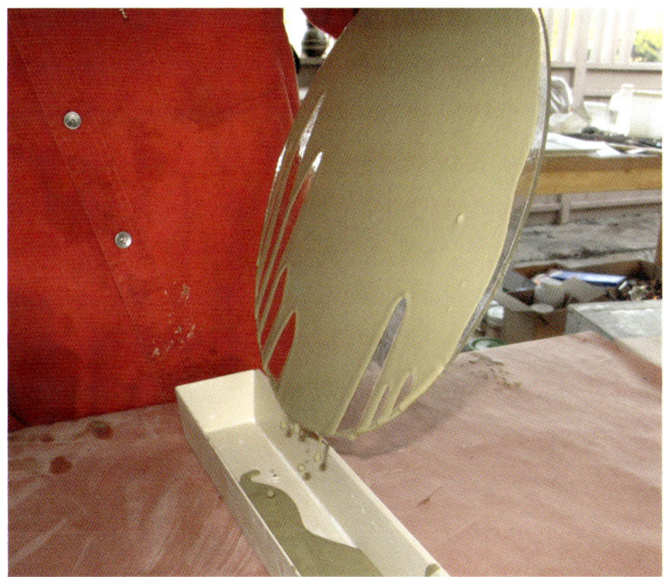

9. *Pouring Reactive enamel as a design to create a basecoat on a 12" glass blank.*

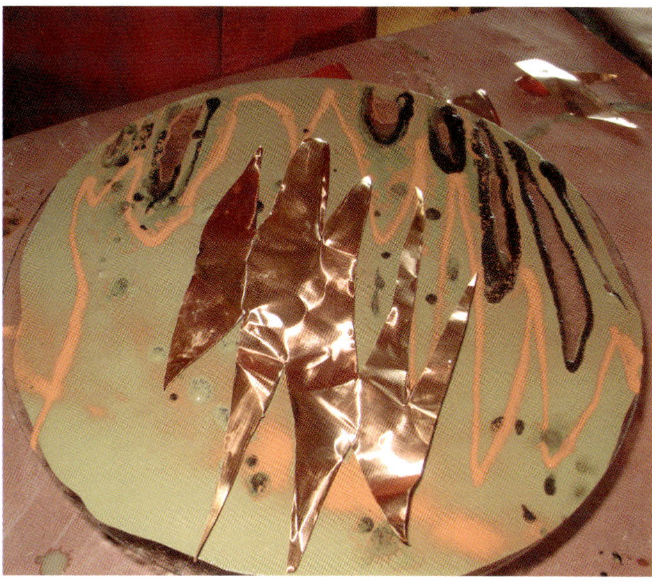

10. *Freeform copper cut-outs mimicking the patterns on the design blank, placed on top of wet enamel.*

the whole piece. Another method is to pour the glaze over the pot and let the excess run back into the container. Reactive Dry Enamels are inexpensive enough to paint, splatter or, as used in this process, pour. Every application will result in a piece of a different character.

In traditional Japanese Raku, the reduction of copper to make iridescent golds, blues and greens was not part of the process. The modern non-traditional Raku process was developed and taught by Paul Soldner and his students at the Claremont Graduate Program in the early sixties. As a student in that program I discovered that copper modified with small amounts of other metal oxides reduces the oxide combinations to form micro crystals in a variety of colors. This is the same as Reactive Dry Enamels used in glass. I have come to see this as a kind of glass Raku.

11. *Completed piece shown in photos 9 & 10, 12" finished disc in commercial display stand.*

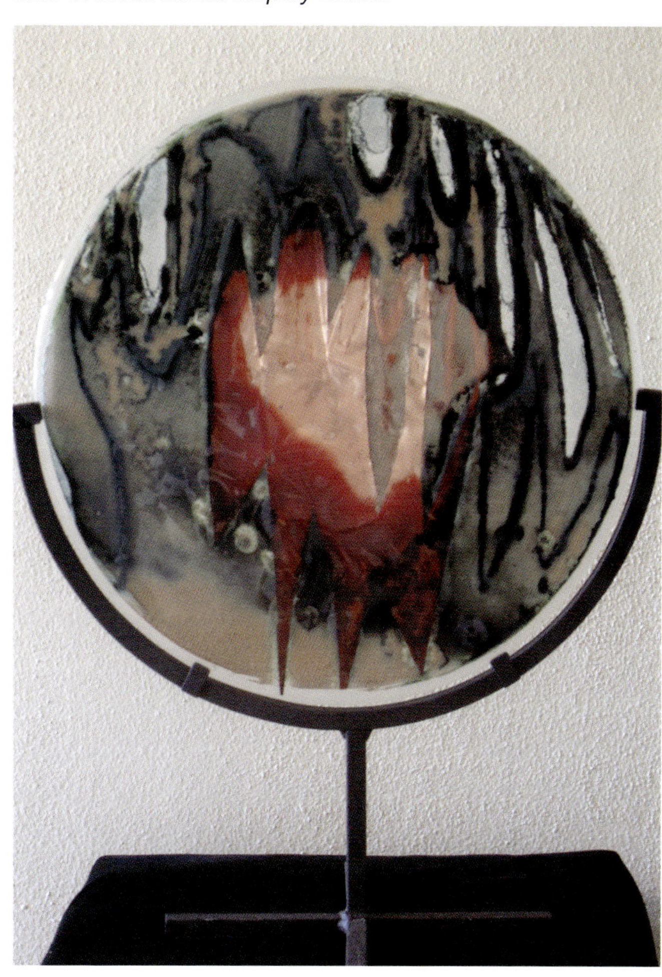

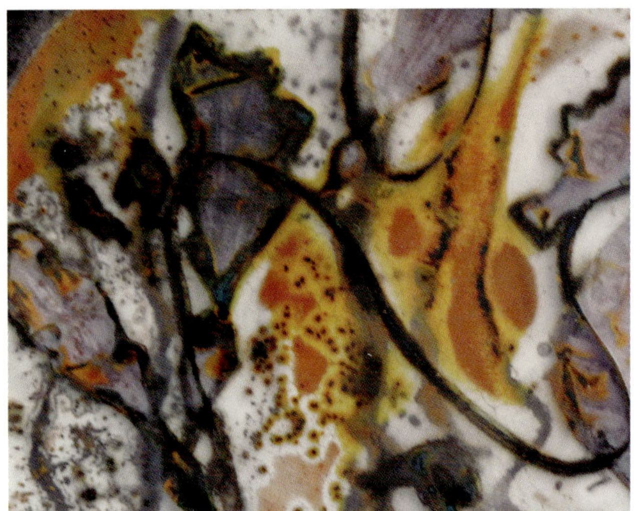

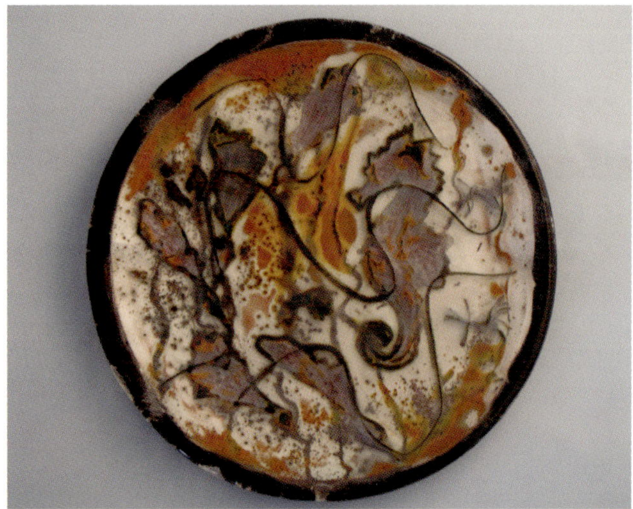

12–13. *The atmosphere between the layers of glass may be changed from place to place on the tile or plate by using Reactive Dry Enamels and reduced copper (copper wire) and copper sulfate.*

Reduction Creates Raku Colors

Reduction is the process of removing oxygen from around an item. In the Raku process this is done at the end of the firing by placing the pot, red hot, into leaves or other organic matter within a closed container. In gas-fired ceramic kilns, adding excess gas to the firing chamber reduces the atmosphere of the whole kiln which reduces the glazes (glass) on the outside of the pot. In an electric fusing kiln, materials that burn (such as briquettes and charcoal) are put into the kiln during the last half of the firing. Both of these reduction methods create an atmosphere so starved of oxygen that oxygen is pulled from any chemically active material present. This is called general atmospheric reduction.

Another method of reduction is being used here, local reduction. Adding organic material or chemicals that suck up oxygen between layers of glass creates a local reduction. Removing the oxygen from the kiln as well as between the glass can enhance process. The metals, copper, iron, silver, brass, change colors when reduced. Chrome and cobalt do not.

Striking

There are several ways that “striking”, or color changing, may occur. Some oxide colors change upon reheating. A copper red glass is clear at the end of the forming process. When this light straw colored glass is reheated to approximately 1300° F, the copper molecules within the glass migrate toward each other, growing larger. When cooled, the larger molecules refract the light differently then before heating, creating copper red glass!

Another form of striking takes place when metals are held within a specific temperature range that is conducive to crystal growth. Micro crystals of copper and other trace metals can make six to eight colors.

When firing Raku clay, the rhythms of the process, the spirit, and the discovery of the unknown, embrace the element of surprise. All these elements are present in the Raku glass process, utilizing the reduction of copper and metal oxides to create mystery in the finished work. Experimenting continues, firing time will shorten, and the action will become more defined.

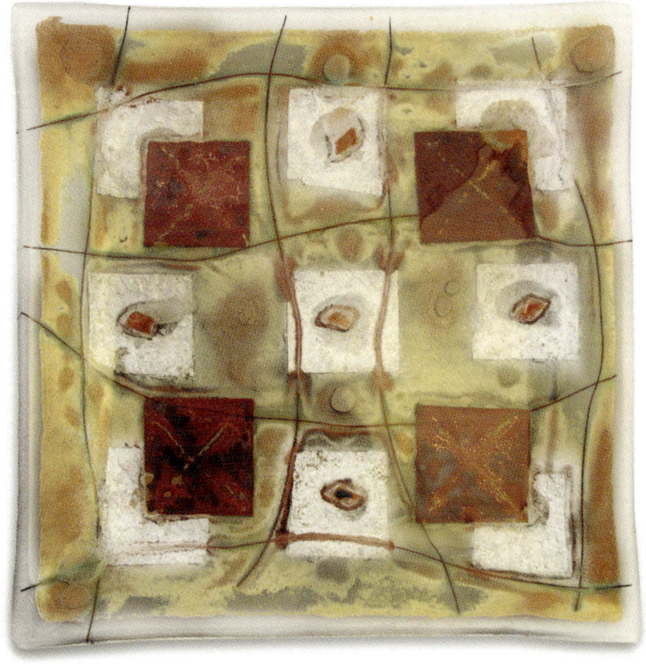

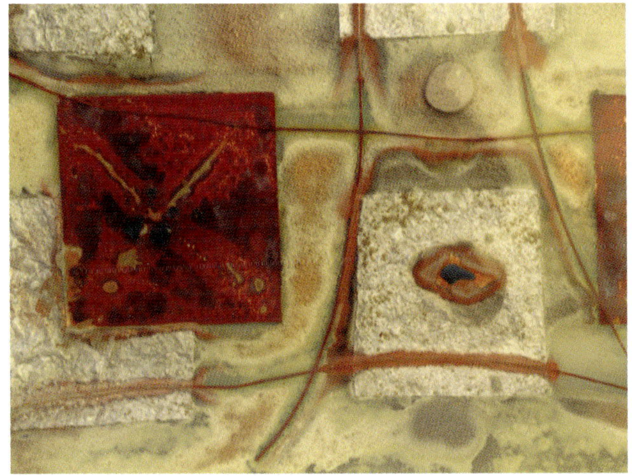

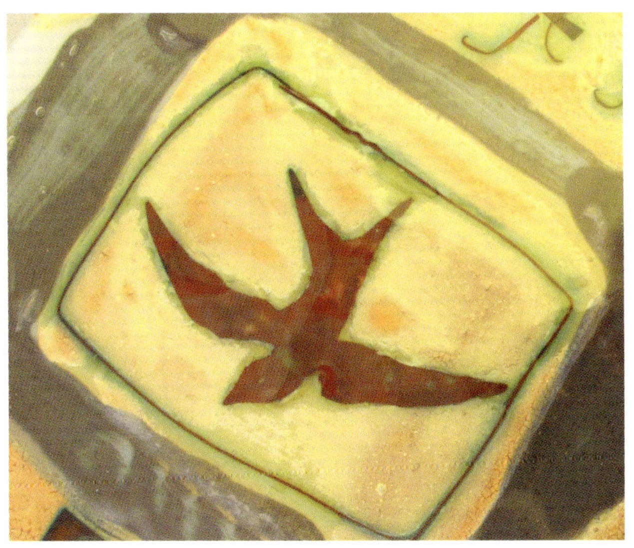

Materials – Dry Enamel

Reactive Dry Enamels are a combination of mined and milled alkaline or acidic earths that contain various salt carbonates, chlorides and sulfates, as well as many trace metals. Green Earth is alkaline when wet. It has a pH of 9.5 to 10. Similar pH materials are Milk of Magnesia at 9.5 to 10pH and household ammonia at 10.5 to 11pH.

The second Reactive Dry Enamel, Brown & Green, is acidic with a pH of 3.5 to 4, very similar to household vinegar and orange juice. As always, you should take care not to splash either of these enamels in your eyes, and remember to wash your hands often. Exposure of the enamel to the copper will change the color and sometimes the texture of the line or shape, depending on the length of exposure. Lines may blur and new lines may be created. The surface may become covered with bubbles. The larger the exposed surface of the copper, the more the reaction. A copper wire will often make a green or brown line, but the edge of a 3 mil copper sheet will only blush green. The variation of responses is due to the amount of surface area being exposed. A wire, for example, has three times the surface area as the edge of a copper sheet of the same gauge. Similarly, a very small diameter copper wire will produce a different color than a larger diameter wire.

14. *Plate, 10" X 10", with geometric design of aluminum & copper foil. The wavy lines that change from green to red do so because Green Earth Reactive Dry Enamel has less access to oxygen in the center of the square plate.*

15. *Close-up showing color change of copper wire and the interface between the copper foil and aluminum foil.*

16. *A small amount of cobalt oxide blue was added to Green Earth Reactive Dry Enamel which surrounds the copper wire that flows shadow green.*

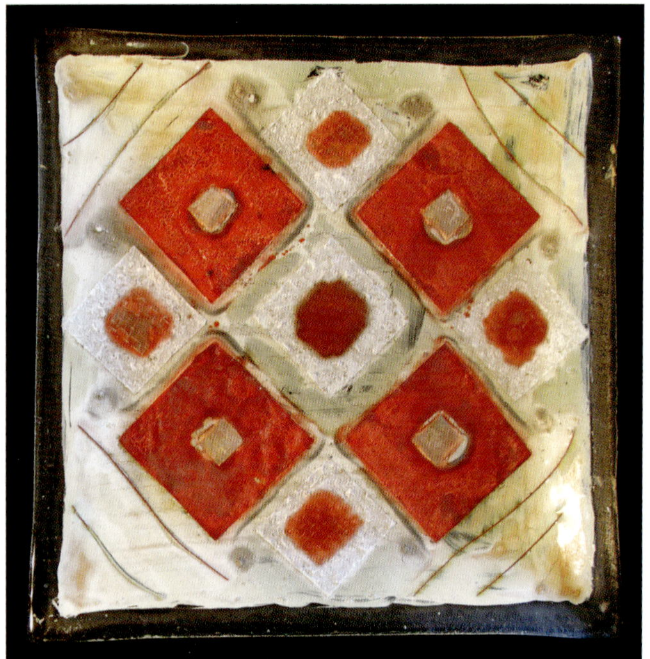

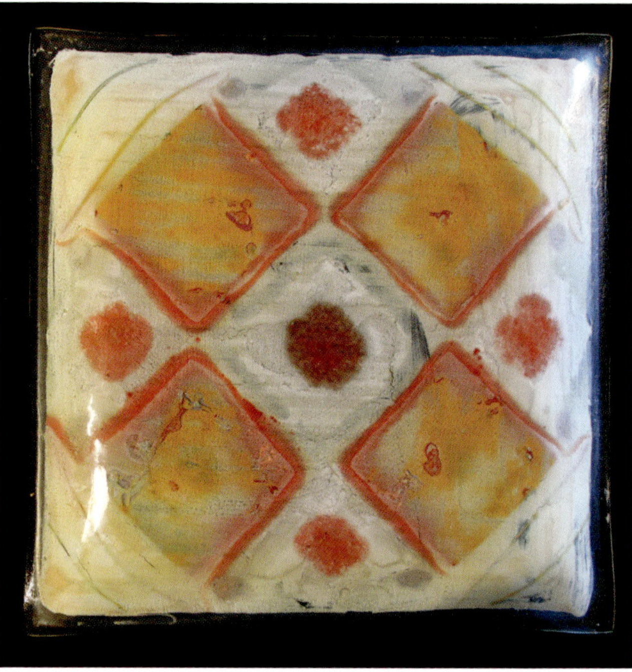

17 - 18. *10" X 10" shallow square plate shown using Green Earth Reactive Dry Enamel from the top and bottom. The chemicals were only allowed to react for 30 minutes before firing, not enough reaction time for the copper to turn green.*

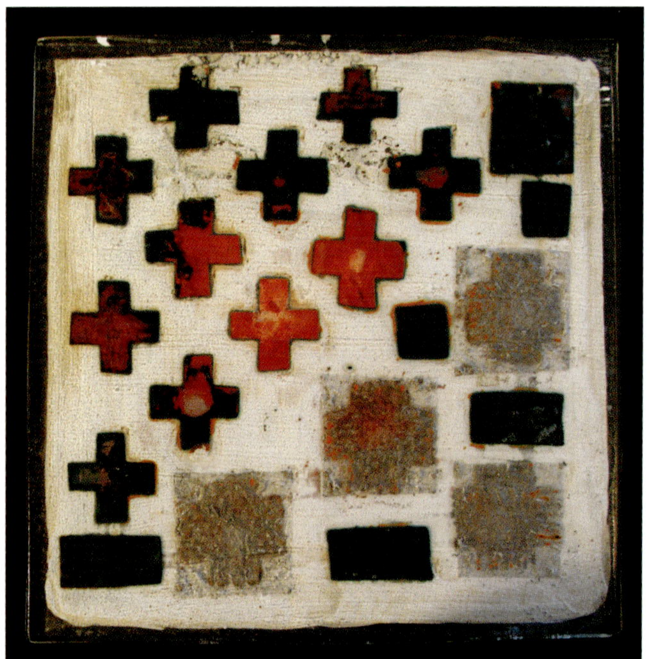

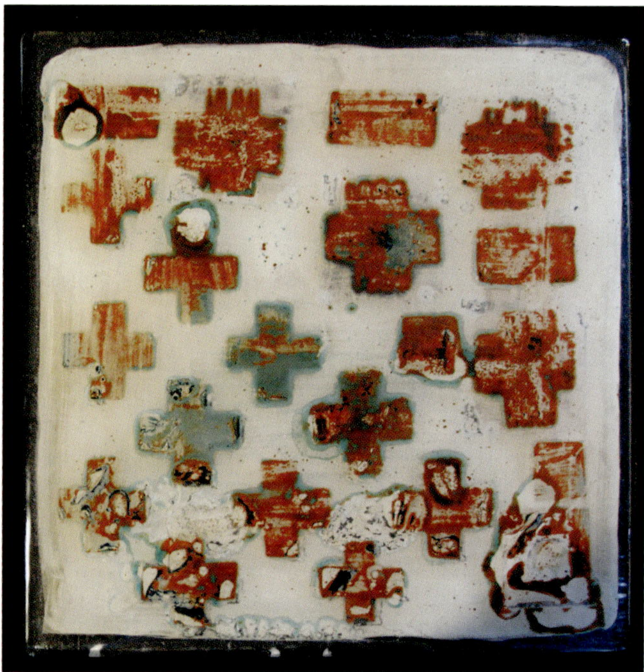

19 - 20. *Flat panel using copper crosses and unwoven copper screen on top of aluminum squares set on Brown & Green Reactive Dry Enamel. Photo #20 shows bottom side of previous panel - reaction time was 2 hrs, giving the copper time to change to green and aqua.*

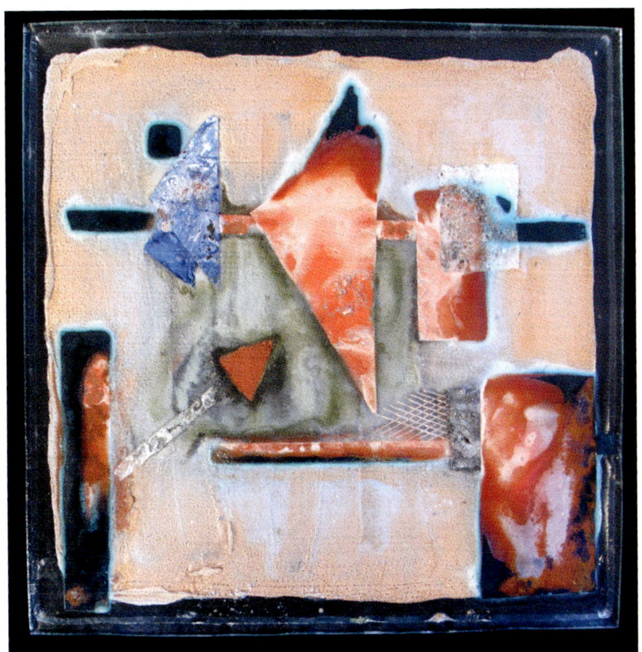

21. *Which side is Up? Green Earth Reactive Dry Enamel with copper elements on float glass. No front, No back, No bubbles.*

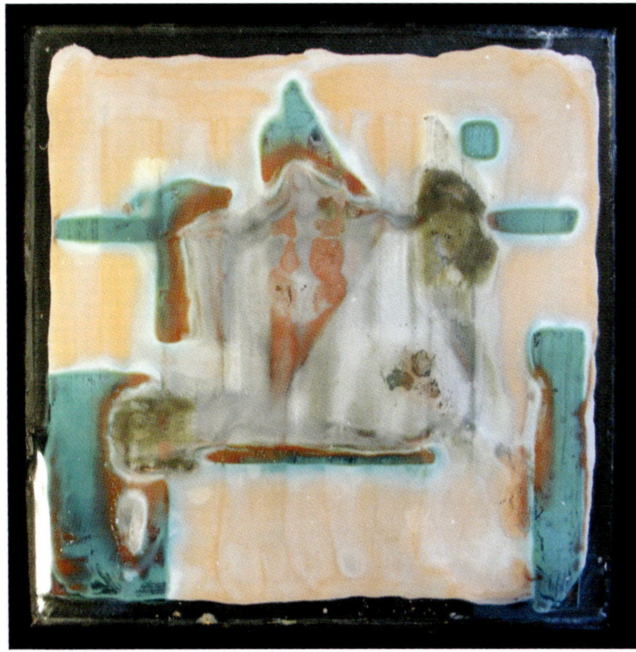

22. *Flip side – Float Glass.*

The Bottom Is The Top

What side is the top? I have asked myself this question since I started using Reactive Dry Enamel coatings and copper. As you can see in the eight photos on these pages, each surface has a distinctively different line structure, a different color, and a different attitude. I deal with it by applying the reactive dry enamel that gives me the line and color quality I think I want, then putting an opal white or black blank on the opposite side. Making the decision as to the side I want , usually makes me feel better, so I'm not continually looking at the bottom. Now I wonder, though, am I missing something? Is there lost beauty hidden forever on the side I have covered?

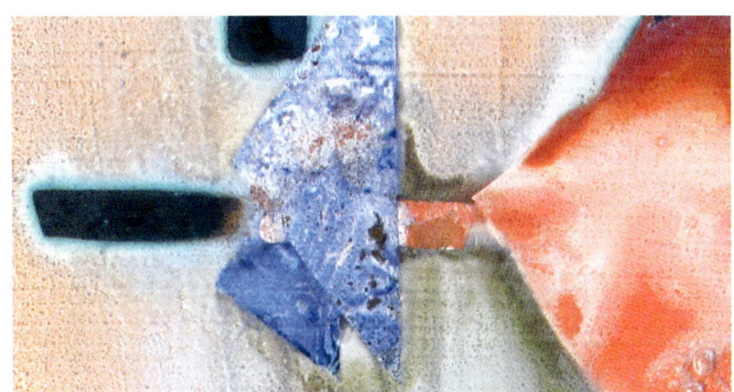

23. *Close-up of the bottom of the piece above, showing the use of Cobalt painted on aluminum prior to being cut.*

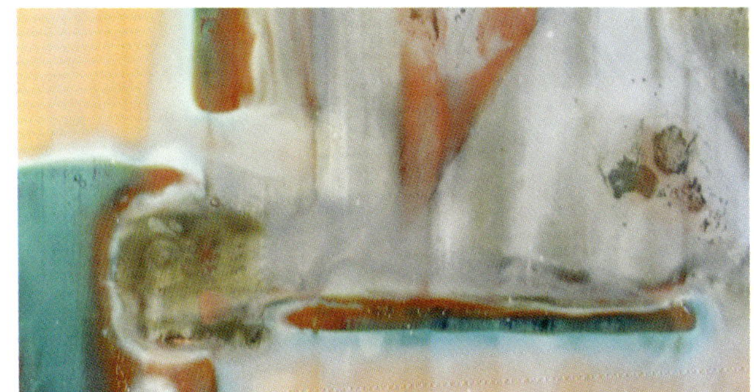

24. *Close-up of Reactive Dry Enamel covering the copper. The 2–hour reactive time allowed the continued action toward aqua.*

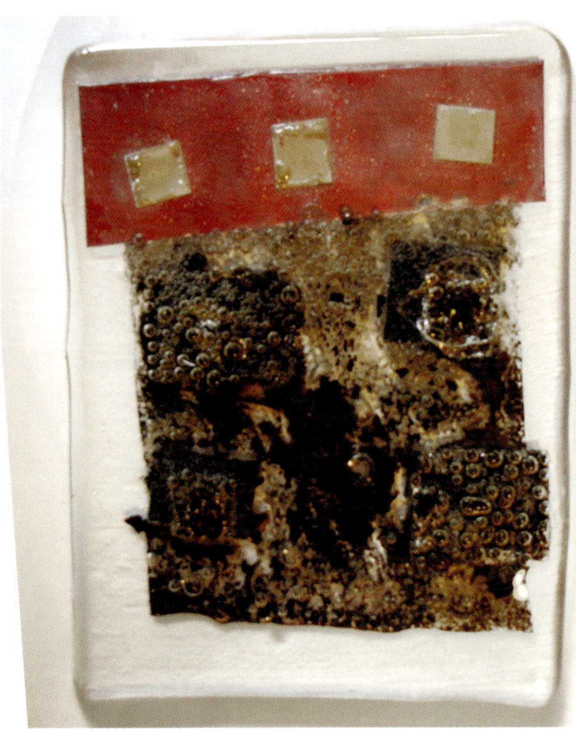

25. ***Float Glass*** *fusing test using small brass squares over copper and three thicknesses of aluminum foil. Fired to 1475° F.*

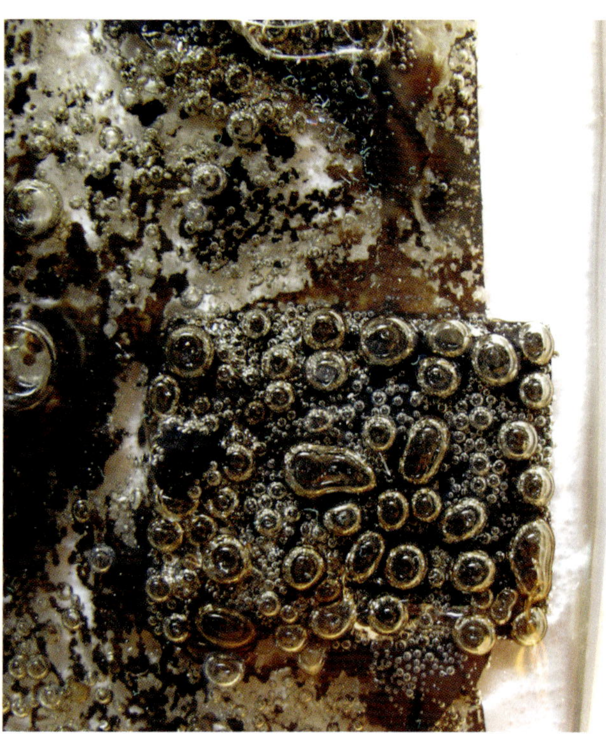

26. *Close-up of bubbles formed on aluminum foil cut from a soft drink can. The bubbles do not rise to the surface because window glass has a high viscosity at 1475° F.*

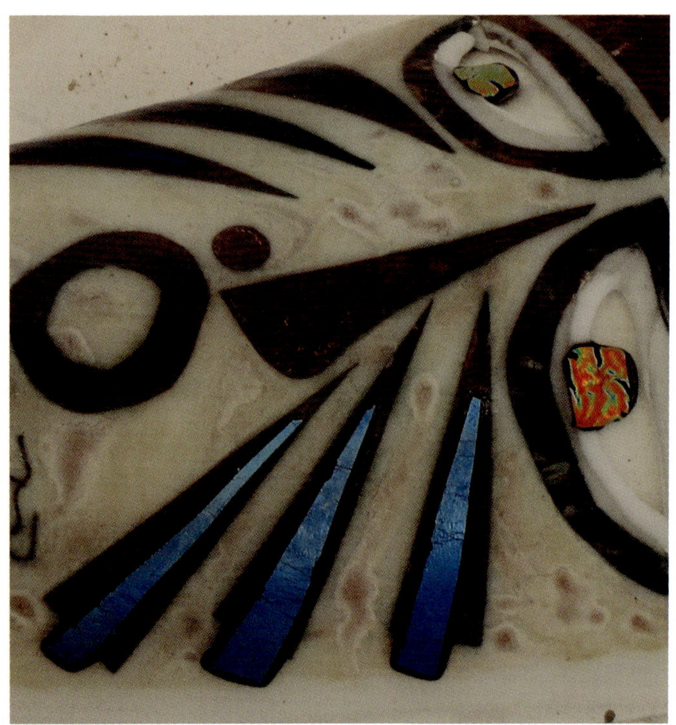

27. *Small accents of dichroic glass on the cheeks of the mask were placed on top of the glass blank; the interior copper acts as an outline shadow.*

Glass Choices

I have chosen to use 1/8" Wissmach 90 COE glass for all the projects in this booklet. It has a moderate viscosity and a longer working range than float glass. All 90 COE glass, such as Uroboros 90 and Bullseye 90, have similar working characteristics.

You can also use float (window) glass and thus lower the cost of your project 50% to 80%. Float glass has a high viscosity, and it melts at a higher temperature. Window glass will work very well for all these processes, though it will change from what you see in this book due to being fired 100° F higher than art glass. The higher temperature affects the chemical reaction. Additionally float glass is stiffer, so

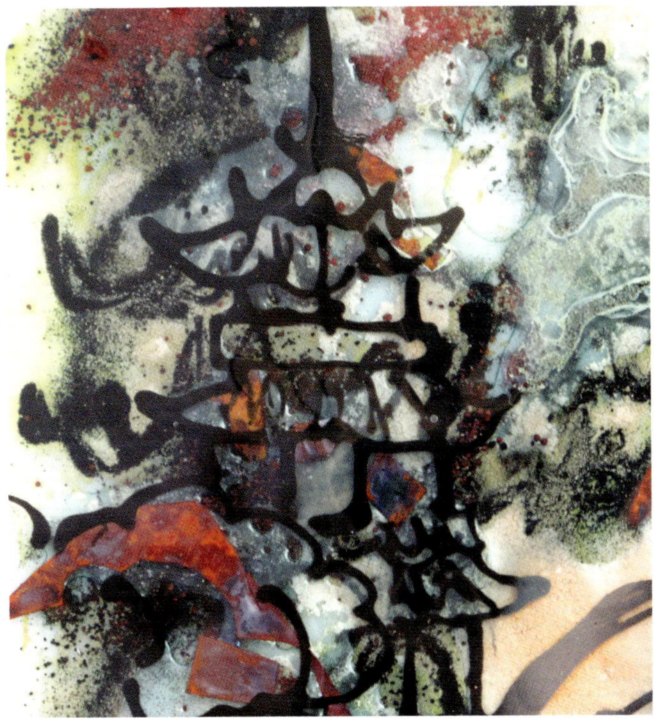

28. *Fine copper powder trailed on dry tile after background copper foil cutouts and copper sprinkles have dried in place.*

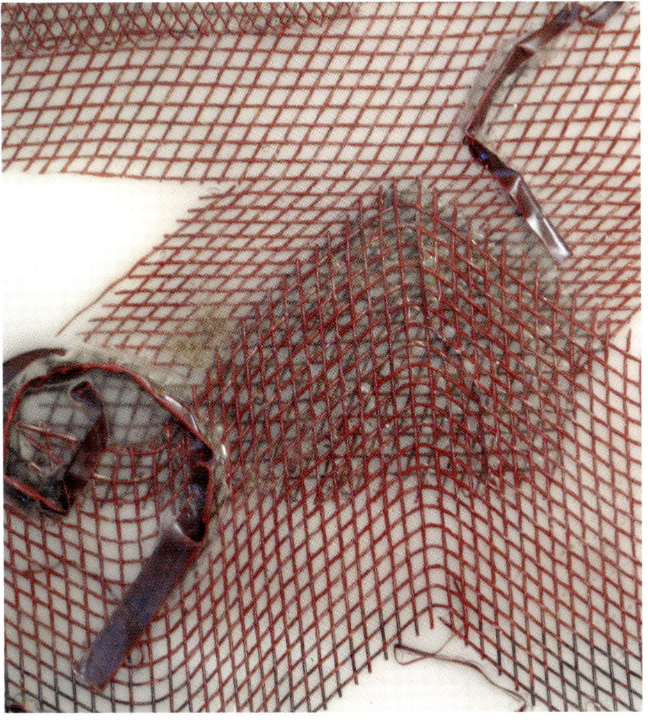

29. *16 gauge wire and large copper mesh screen that has been reformed by stretching cut ribbons.*

the bubbles that form from out-gassing of the inclusions are smaller and do not rise to the surface. EZ Fuse glass that fits float, made by Youghiogheny, comes in colors and black and white, so you can choose to have a colored background.

Copper Choices

Copper sheet, foil, wire, filings, and of course mesh, are all available from hobby glass sources and are all viable inclusions. Some scrubbies found in the kitchen department are copper. I have used 1/2″ copper plumbing fittings for candleholders, copper nails for cactus, etc. I could go on and on.

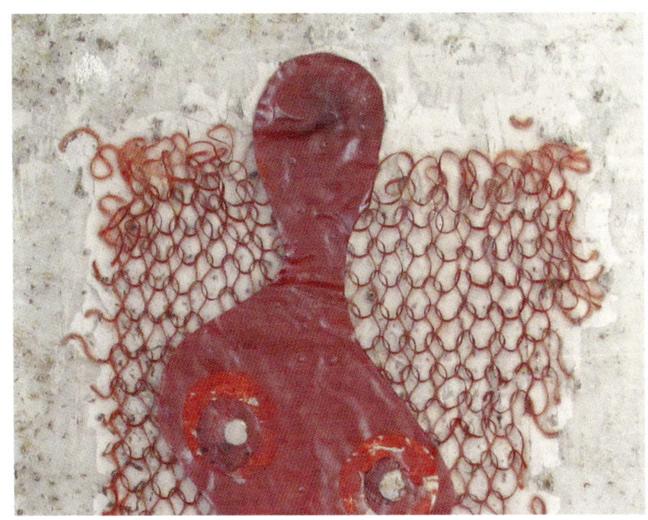

30. *An unraveled copper scrubbie, used for the background texture.*

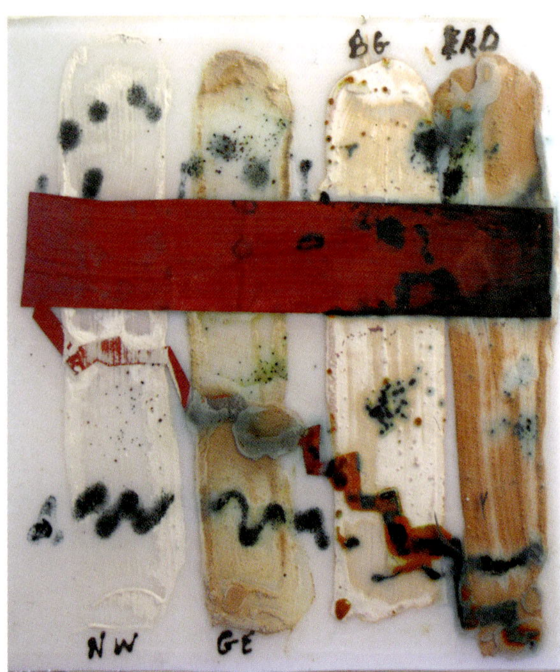

31. *Test tile showing a side-by-side comparison of White Linen, Green Earth, Brown & Green, and a mix of red dirt and fireplace ash.*

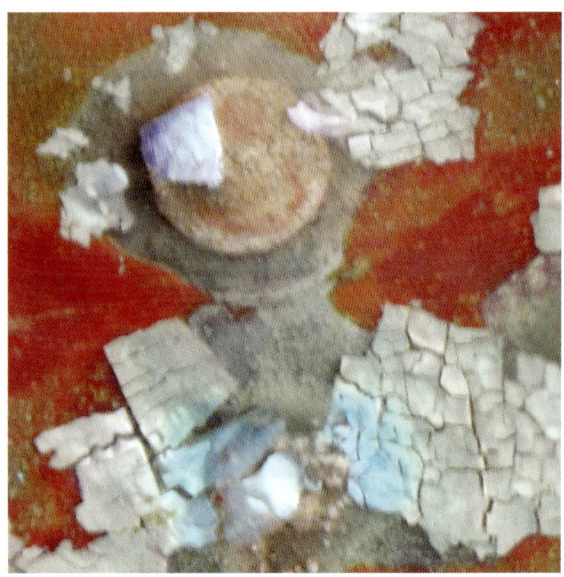

33. *Very close-up. Dichroic confetti made by CBS. The small flakes are used as sprinkles over any material and when fired, change color due to the angle of the light.*

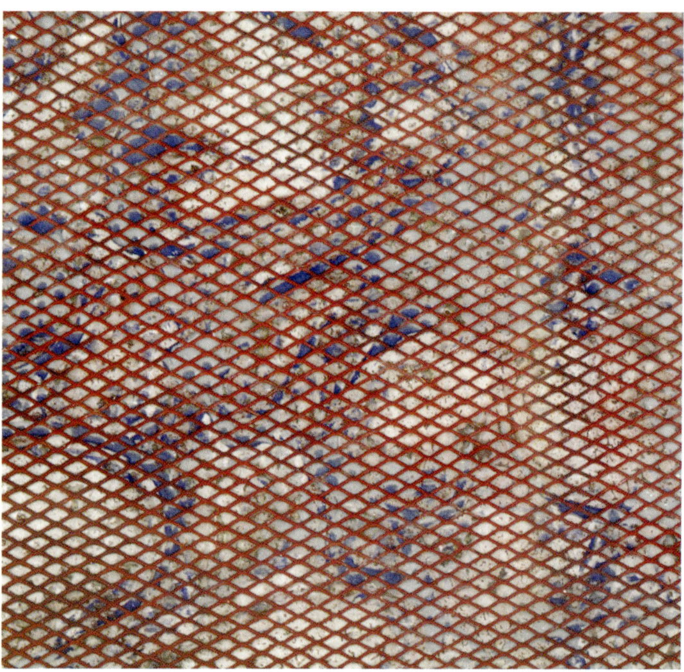

32. *Diamond mesh screen covering Cobalt Blue and White Linen Dry Enamel on aluminum foil. Diamond mesh copper screen is made from one piece of copper so it is not possible to unweave like woven screen. Double the diamond mesh and create a moiré pattern.*

Copper powder of various meshes can be used in a variety of processes. Try heating copper powder in your kiln to 650 degrees F for 15 minutes; it will turn into black copper oxide, resulting in a different color on the outer surface in the final fusing.

Brass is approximately 85% copper plus the addition of both zinc and tin. Brass is a great addition to the color palette of metals. Brass shim stock of 3 to 5 mil thickness can be purchased from a hardware or auto parts store. Though stiff and hard, it will submit to a good pair of KitchenAid scissors. Brass wire is also available at many hardware stores. Because brass contains varying amounts of copper and zinc, distinctive colors from copper result when used with Reactive Dry Enamels.

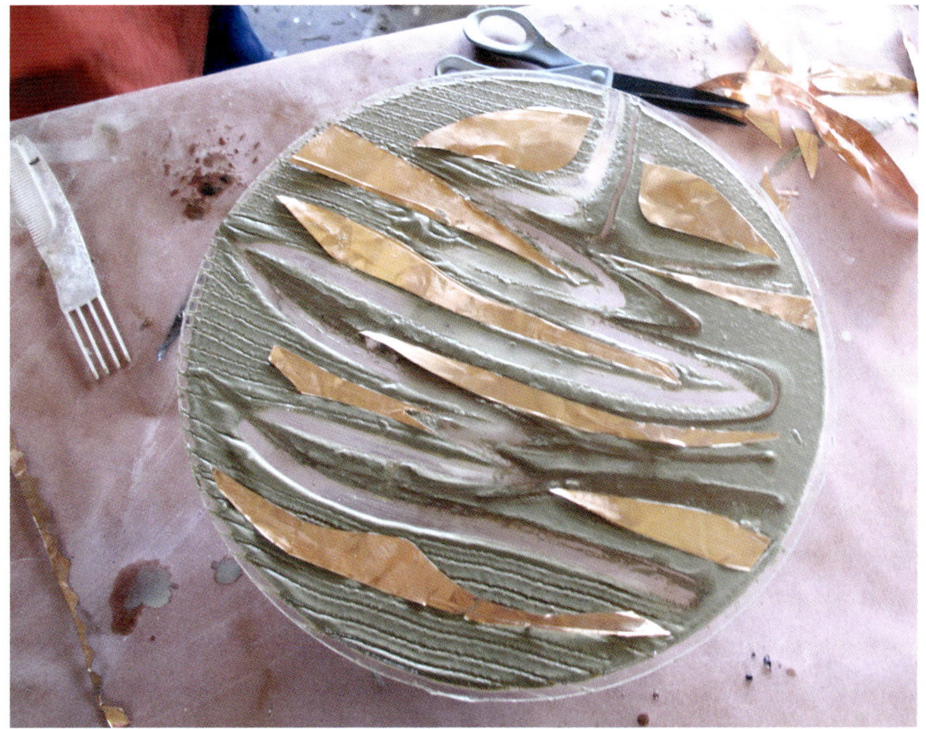

34. *Close up of plate with finger drawing, cut copper pieces and combed enamel background.*

Mixing and Application of Reactive Dry Enamels

Reactive Dry Enamels may be mixed with each other or with White Linen Reactive Dry Enamel. When blending any of Boyce Lundstrom Reactive Dry Enamels and mixing with water, a reaction that creates gas will make the combination puff and change texture. This reaction looks a lot like yeast when it reacts with sugar. After 10 to 15 minutes, add a small amount of water and stir vigorously until the carbonation disappears. As explained earlier, one Reactive Dry Enamel is acid earth and one is alkali earth. So when mixing Brown & Green with Green Earth, you are mixing materials like lemon juice and baking soda—which are acid and base—and they erupt. This mix of Reactive Dry Enamels, now called " Razzle Dazzle," is responsible for an uncontrolled reaction with metals. Yahoo Raku!

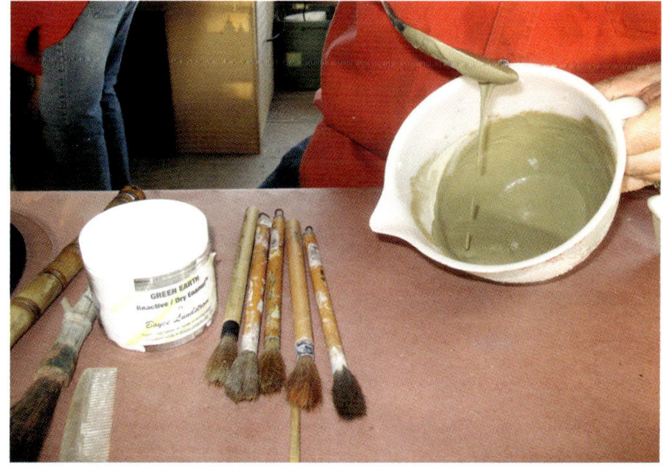

35. *Mix Reactive Dry Enamels in a large measuring cup. Let stand, then add a little water and remix.*

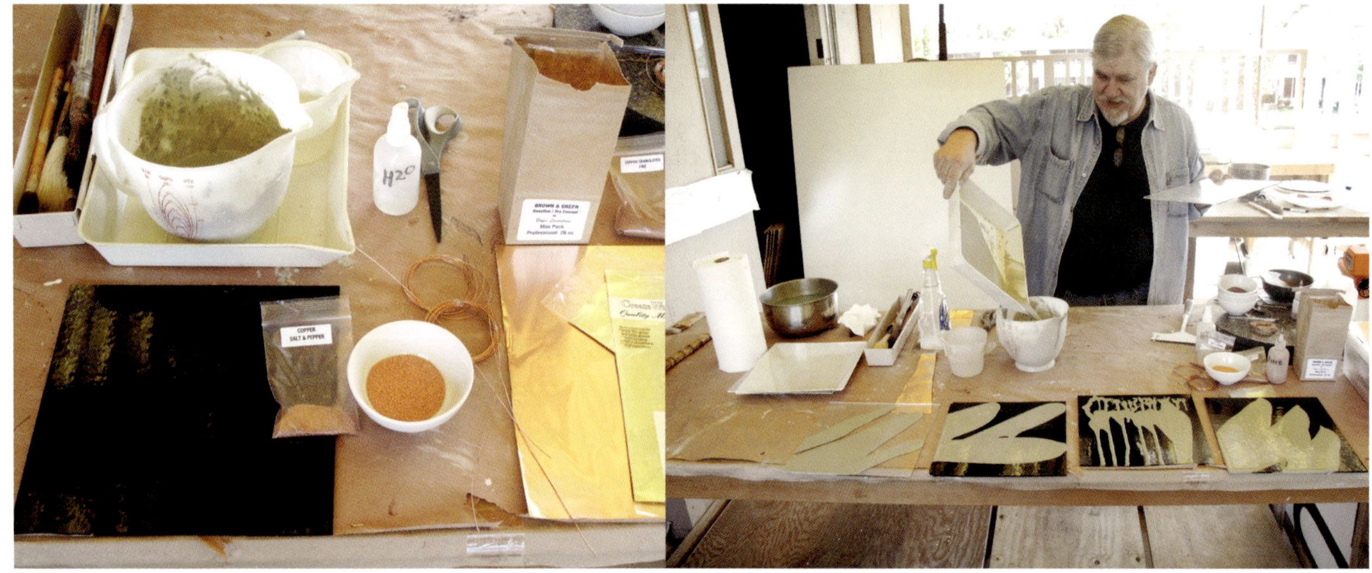

36. *Getting started. Table layout with six materials. Keep it simple by starting with a limited palette of materials.*

37. *It only takes a few moments to pour many designs. The unwanted designs can be squeegeed into different designs.*

Process As Design Method

It is very hard to design 'cold turkey.' Working up a design requires a creative urge that rarely appears on demand. If you set up your workbench with an assortment of materials and use them in a spontaneous way, painting and pouring them on a glass blank (canvas) puts a knife in the heart of that cold turkey.

The photos show a set-up with a limited palette of materials. By limiting the materials and proceeding in a relatively orderly process, one can recall the steps it took to create the line or the effect. I like this better than writing the steps down.

The photos show four application processes: pouring, sponging, spraying and splashing. The consistency of the Reactive Dry Enamel can be changed by adding water and/or CMC. The equipment stands on its own; look what's on the table. I hope it gives you a feeling that anything will work, because it will, nothing special here.

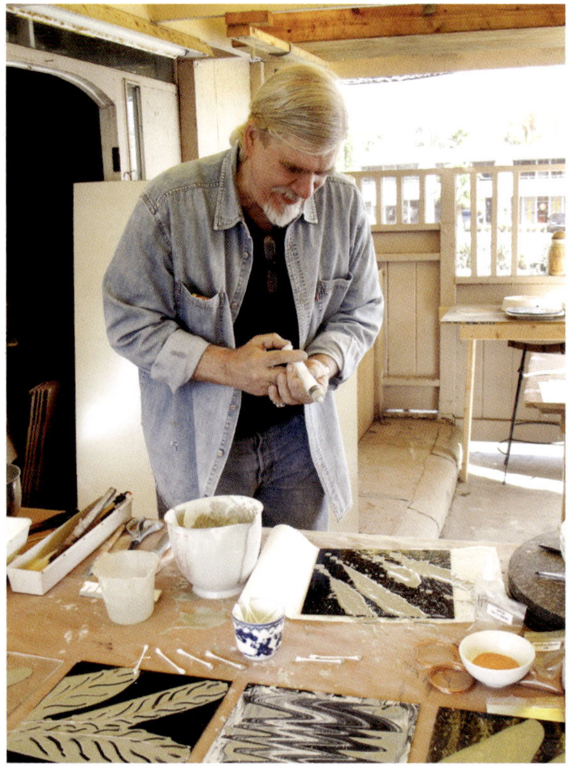

38. *Splattering a design with a large syringe usually used for basting a chicken breast.*

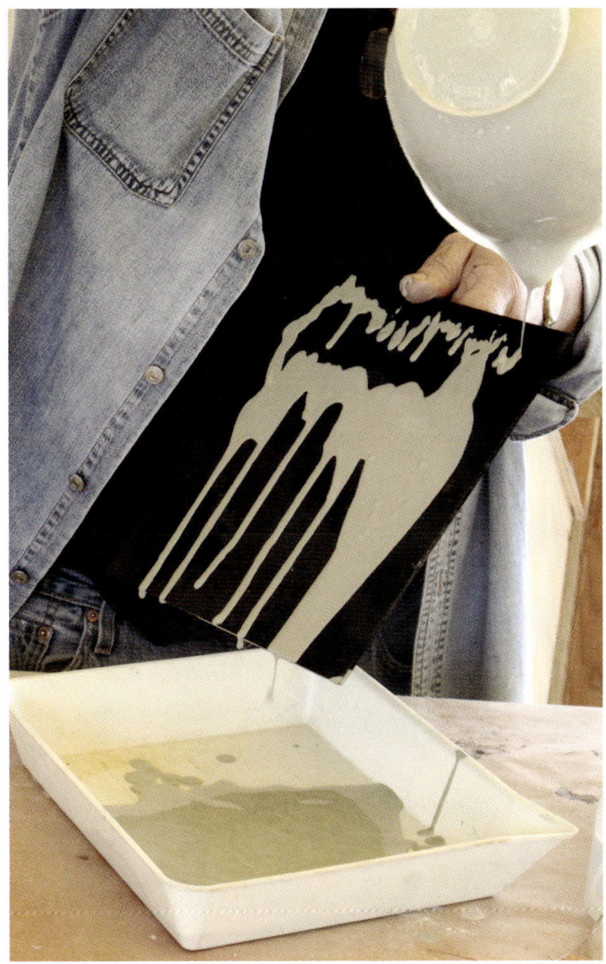

39. *Dripping over a tray with a pour spout. These trays can be purchased from photo equipment suppliers.*

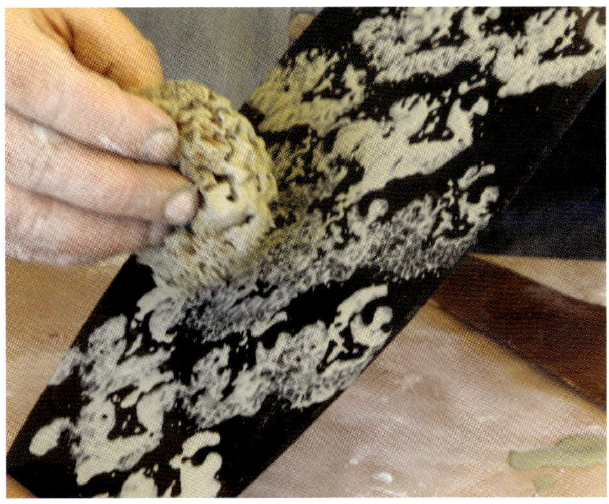

40. *Using a natural sponge to apply a random base coat. Sponge purchased from cosmetic department.*

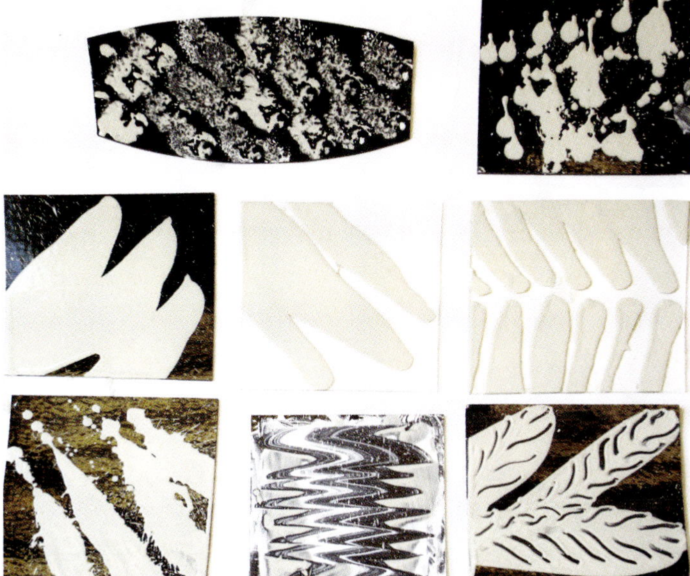

41. *Completed series of glass blanks using five different methods of application.*

The first project for Raku glass is designed to fit a square plate mold. I found this 10 1/4" glazed plate in my cupboard. After cutting two – 10 1/ 4" squares of glass, I sanded the edges to avoid future finger lacerations. Again, the photos tell the story of the process better than any explanation.

I am using Brown & Green Reactive Dry Enamel with water only, no CMC. I started with mixing eight ounces of enamel to a heavy cream consistency, then applying the enamel to eight glass blanks. Then I chose to continue with four of the best designs.

The molds chosen for all projects are simple, functional shapes purchased from Slumpy's or a second-hand store. The molds were also chosen for size; a 10 1/4" square is the largest square that will fit in a seven–sided Skutt 110 volt kiln. And, as we know, BIGGER IS BETTER. You will need a 10.5" square shelf. Of course it is always possible to fuse by placing the piece on the bottom of your kiln lined with a piece of fiber paper.

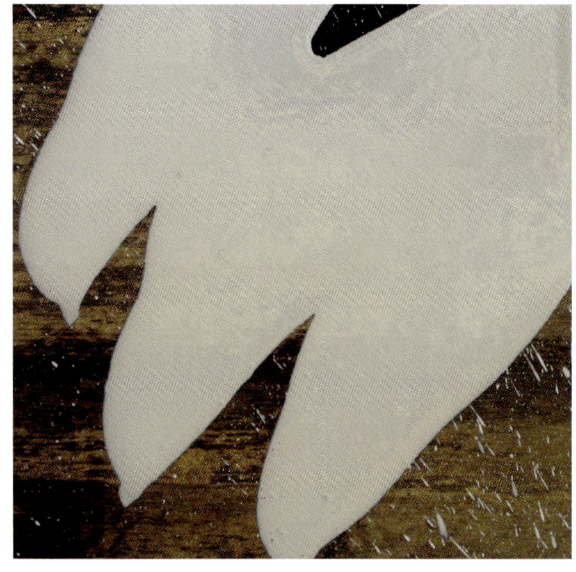

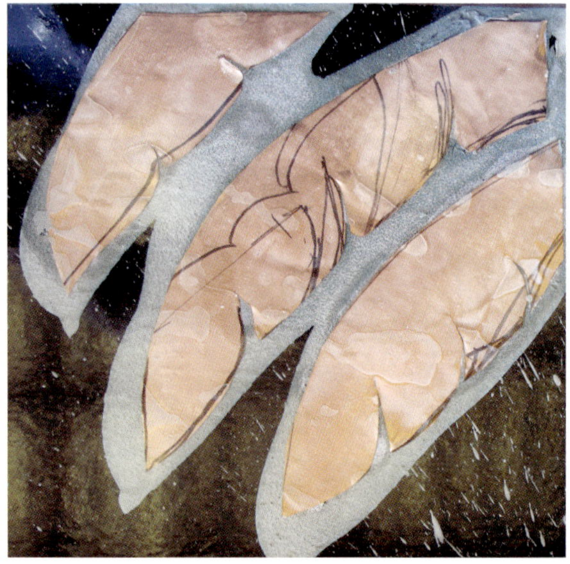

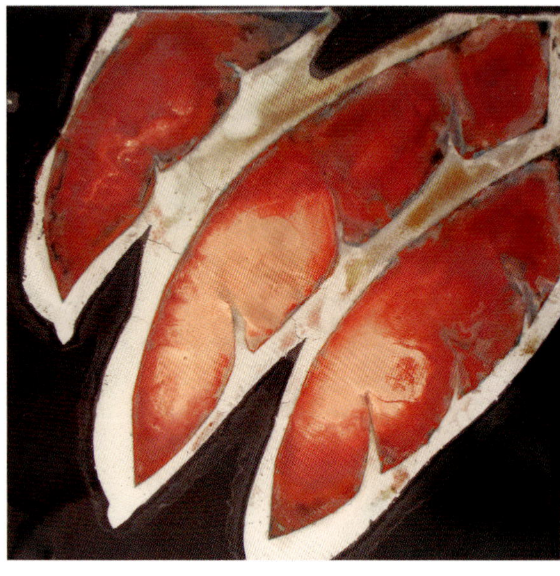

Application Pouring

A picture is worth a thousand words, so look at the pictures. Add water to get the pouring consistency you want and pour a design on the glass blank. If you don't like what you see, scrape it off into your container and re-mix before pouring again.

Now, using the pour lines and the clear areas for inspiration, cut copper foil to cover some of the enamel. Then, among other techniques, use a squirt bottle filled with copper powder to outline the pour marks, creating a pattern.

Slip trailing with glazes—Glassline, copper powder, or Reactive Dry Enamels —is a technique borrowed from ceramics. Since bisque clay pots are absorbent, they hold well-defined lines. But on glass, with its non-absorbent surface, the line tends to spread. You can compensate for this tendency, however, by varying the consistency of the slip material—adjusting the proportions of powder, water and CMC binder. Here are a few pointers to show some of the diverse combinations and percent variations that will give you a stronger sense of control over such variables as color, line, texture, etc. There are potentially thousands of combinations of materials.

42. *Brown & Green Reactive Dry Enamel poured on black glass.*

43. *The copper sheet was drawn and cut out after the enamel was poured.*

44. *Tile 10" X 10" fired twice; first firing to full fuse, second firing to strike (change) the color.*

45-49. *The process showing the steps taken to make a 10" X 10" cactus tile. After pouring the Brown & Green Reactive Dry Enamel, the design was drawn on with a cotton swab, moving the slip, but not removing it.*

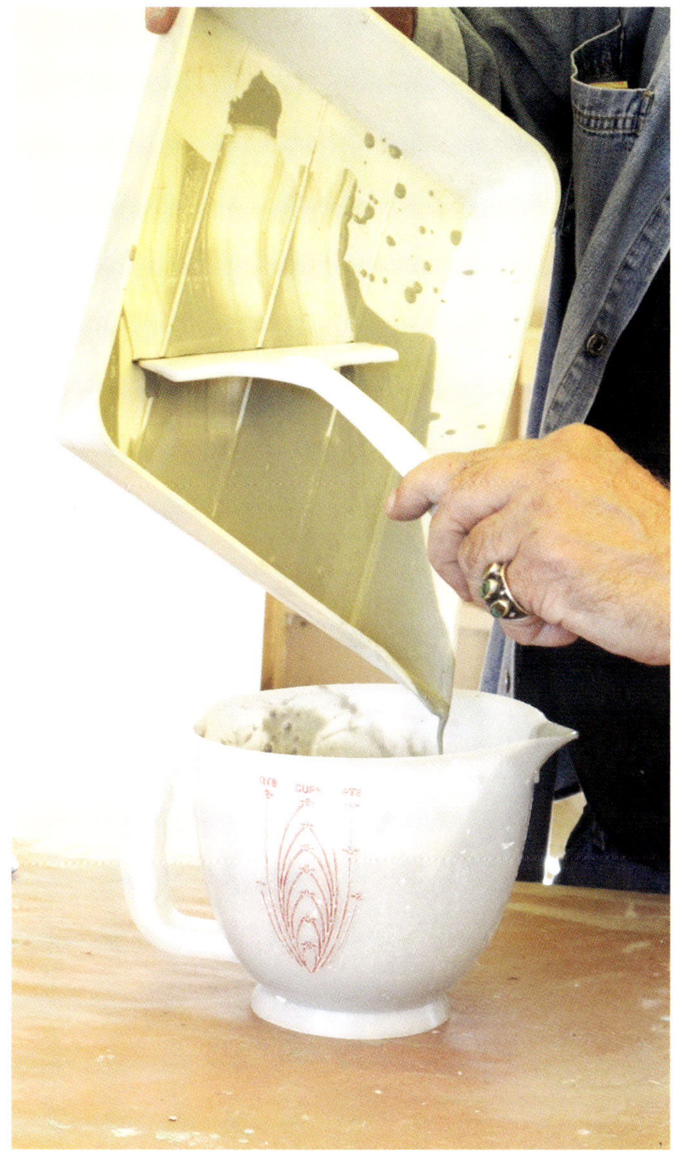

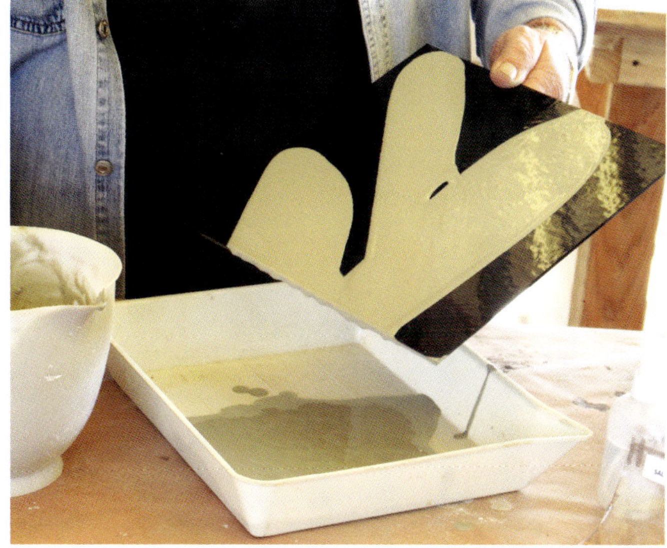

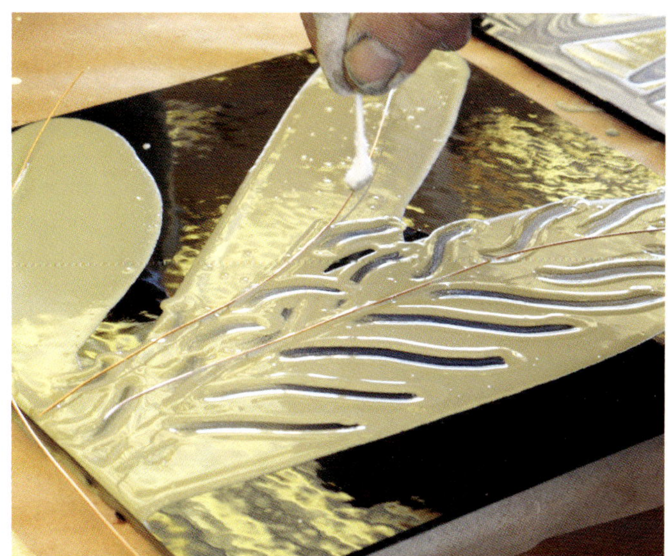

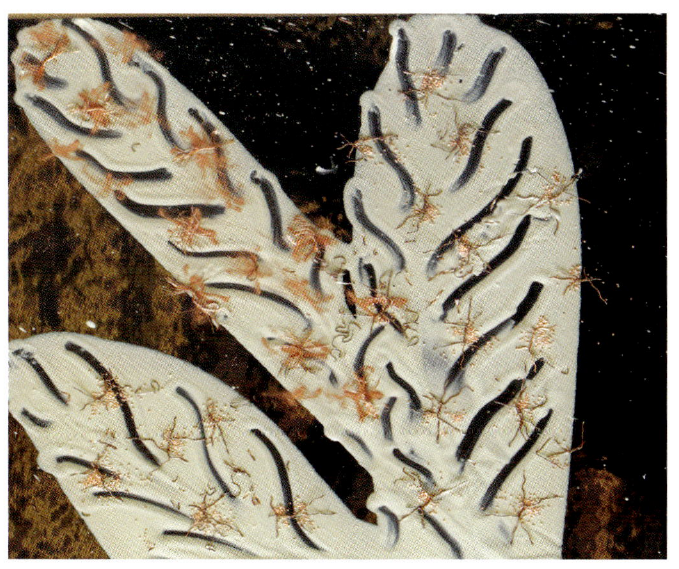

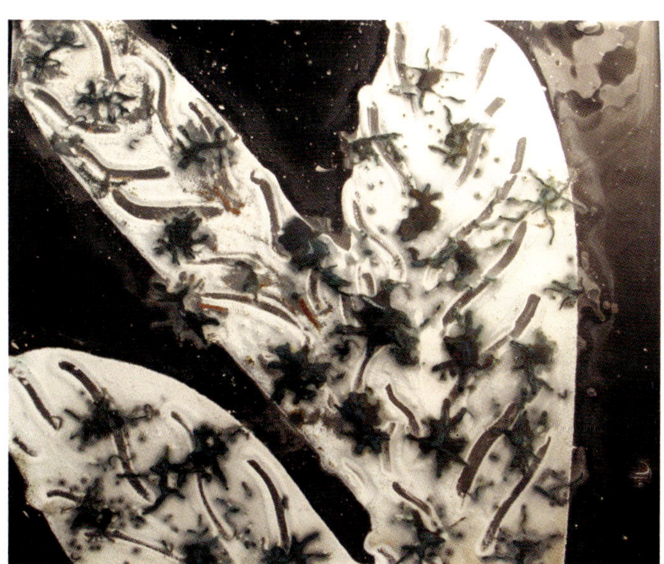

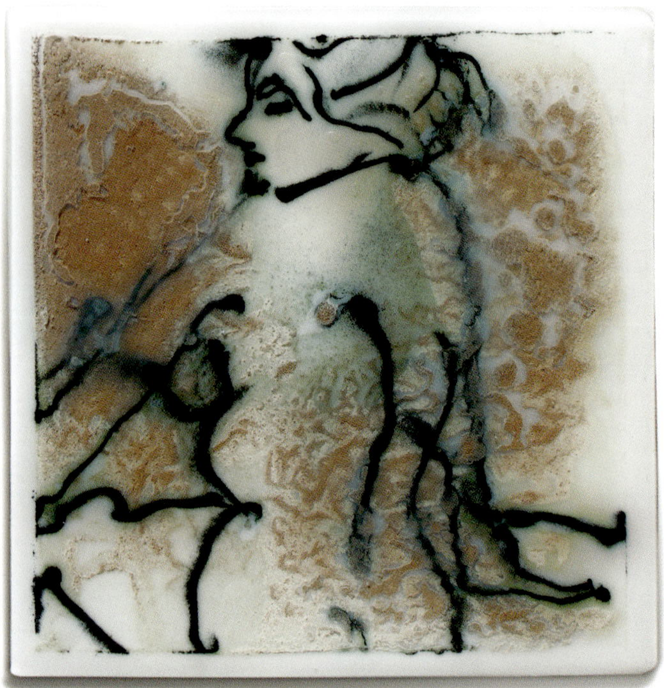

50. *Poured background design created the inspiration for the placement of the nude. Note the green bloom in the center of the tile. This is created by 'puffing' the fine copper powder over wet Reactive Dry Enamel and letting it fall naturally.*

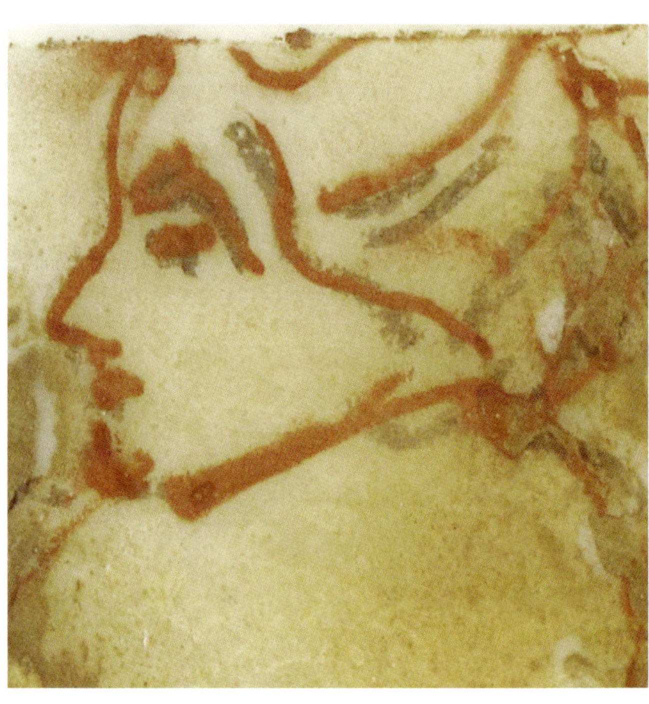

51. *Close-up of previous piece, before firing, showing the dry powder line drawn over the wet slip. Note the variations of thick and thin application.*

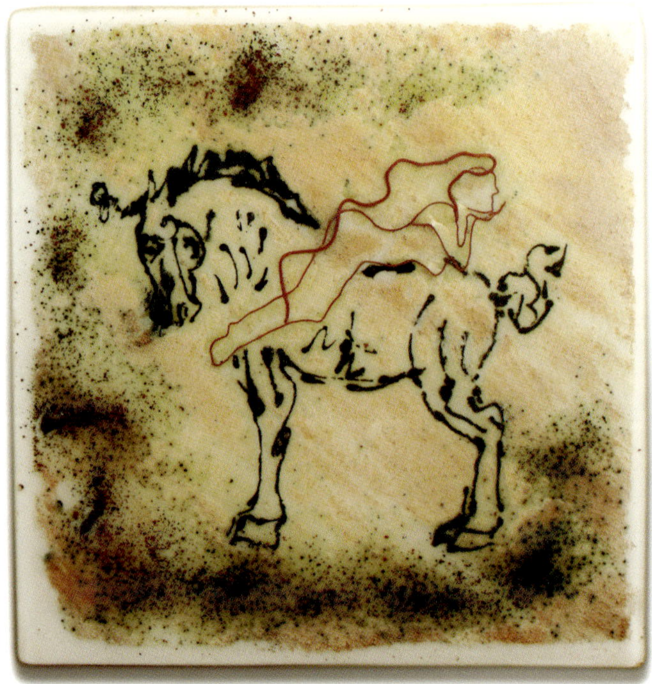

52. *Background of Lady Godiva is sprinkled large particles of copper; half of the Copper Granules were pre-fired to oxidize the surface. This gives both red and green texture shading.*

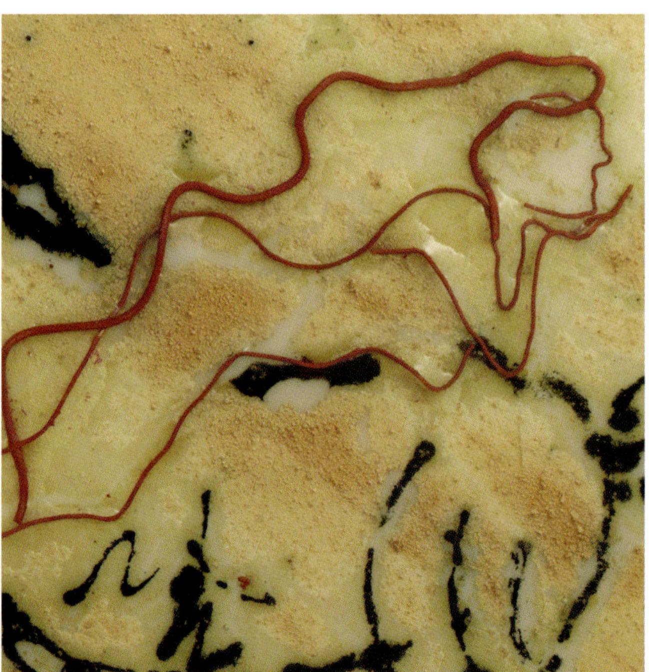

53. *Close-up of Lady Godiva on the back of her horse. Pre-fired copper wire of two different gauges was bent for her figure. Horse drawn with wet copper powder mixed with CMC & water: 1 powder to 5 CMC solution.*

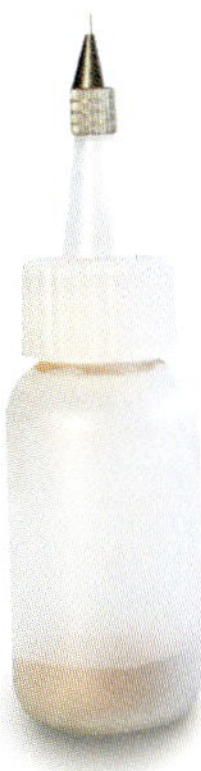

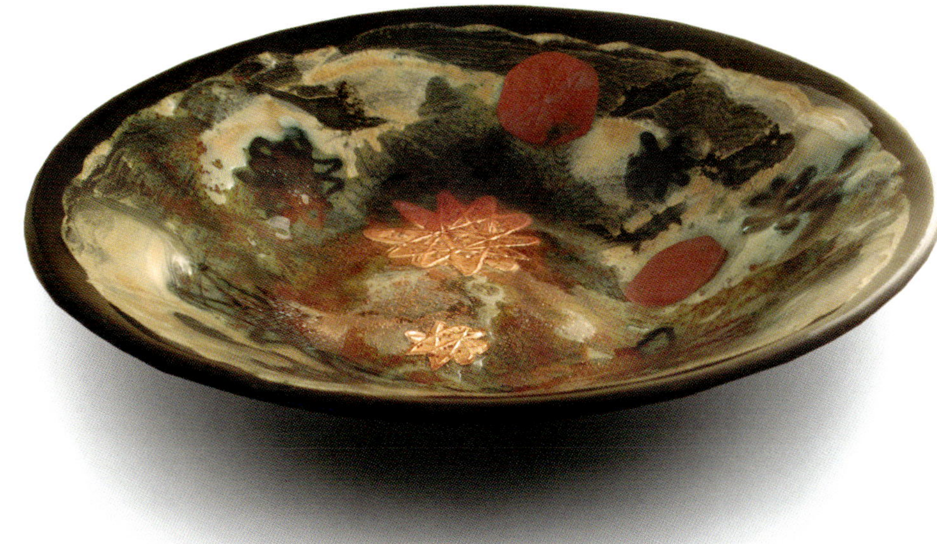

Application Trailing

Trailing is a method of applying thick, creamy liquids, referred to as 'slip', onto a surface. We are applying these liquids with a plastic squeeze bottle using a variety of tips. Possibilities:

1. Dry micron copper will flow without any liquid, trailed through the smallest of tips. For a fine, dark green line, mix copper powder with CMC in various ratios: 1 powder to 4 CMC solution by volume; 1 powder to 6 CMC solution, etc.
2. When adding a reducing agent such as graphite to the copper, or heating the copper before mixing with CMC, the color will change.
3. The slip trailing may be over a pre-applied Reactive Dry Enamel (applied wet then dried) or applied to one blank and then flipped and applied to the wet Reactive Dry Enamel.

To start the reaction between copper and the ground coat, apply dry powder colors over Reactive Dry Enamels and then spray with water. Soon after completing your lay-up, cover the bottom blank and its wet enamel and design elements, with the clear top blank.

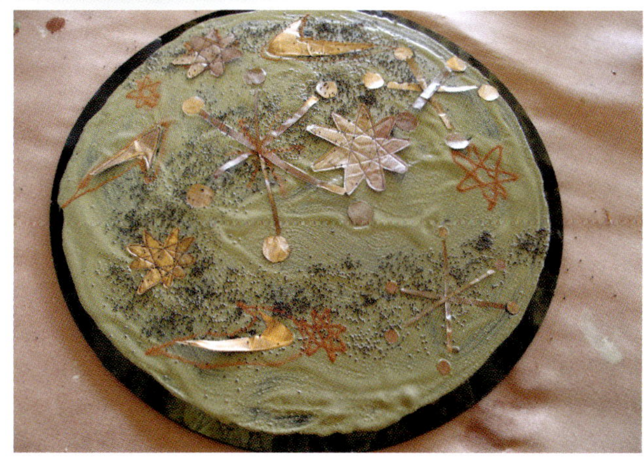

54. *Green Earth was applied with a brush. Cut out symbols of our atomic age were placed on the wet slip.*

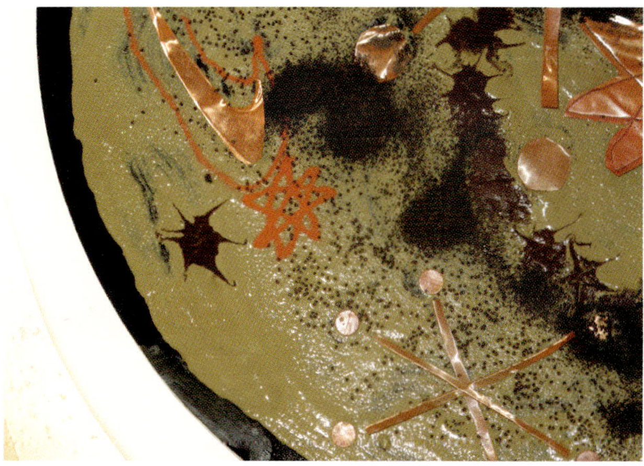

55. *Dry fine copper granules were trailed from a small plastic squeeze bottle using a fine tip to contrast the cut out copper. Finished piece above.*

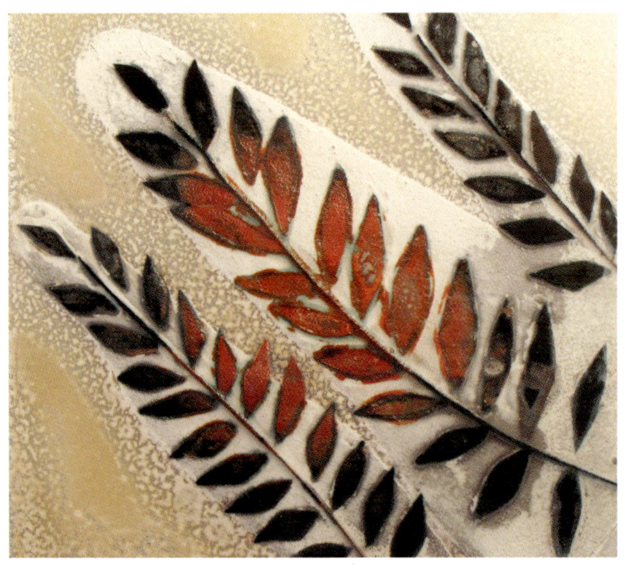

56. *Close-up of pour application with an overspray of the same Reactive Dry Enamel.*

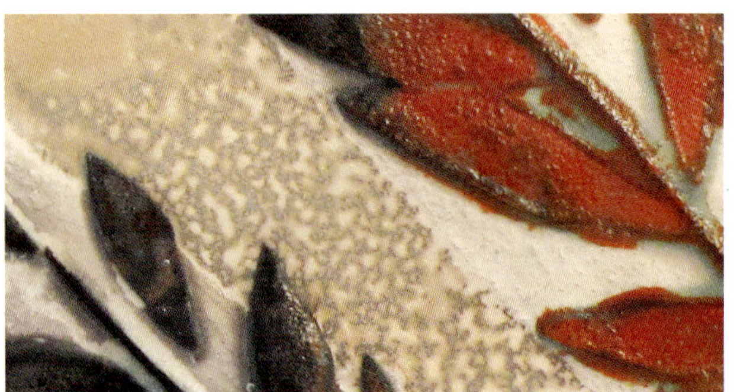

57. *Close-up of photo #56.*

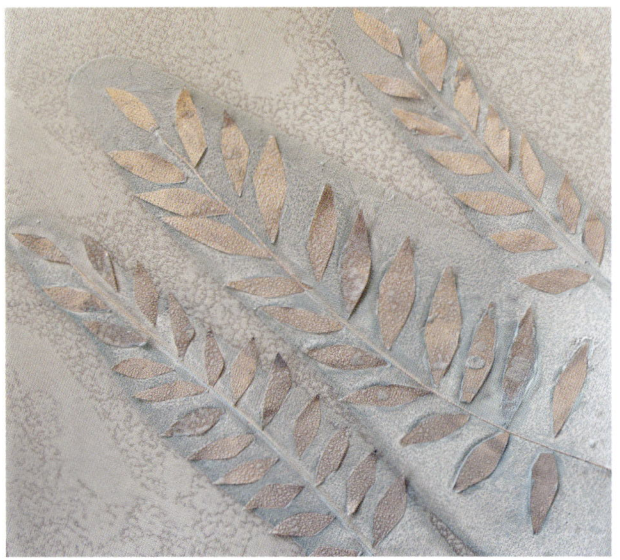

58. *Design after pouring slip, applying copper & foil leaves, then overspraying the entire piece.*

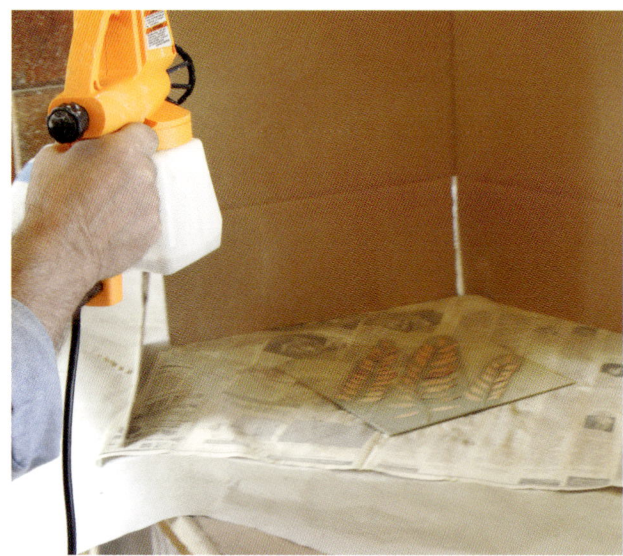

59. *The Dry Enamel was thinned by adding approximately 29% more water and sprayed over the entire surface. Later the edges were cleaned.*

Spray Choices

Overspray. Sooner or later you will want to overspray your entire piece to hold powdered enamels or dry copper granular application in place. Spray water over Reactive Dry Enamels during the construction process if your studio is warm or if you are working outside in a breeze. First choice for sprayers is a mouth spray siphon. It's always handy, easy to use and easy to clean. Next choice is compressed air from a can or pump; they are easy to keep handy at the bench and relatively inexpensive.

Most recently I've been using a modified garden sprayer. This is consistent with my conviction that you can find most materials from the hardware store or Home Depot or other local venders instead of from art supply stores. I bought an electric spray gun from my favorite-of-all-equipment stores, Harbor Freight, with its cheap made-in-China

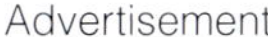

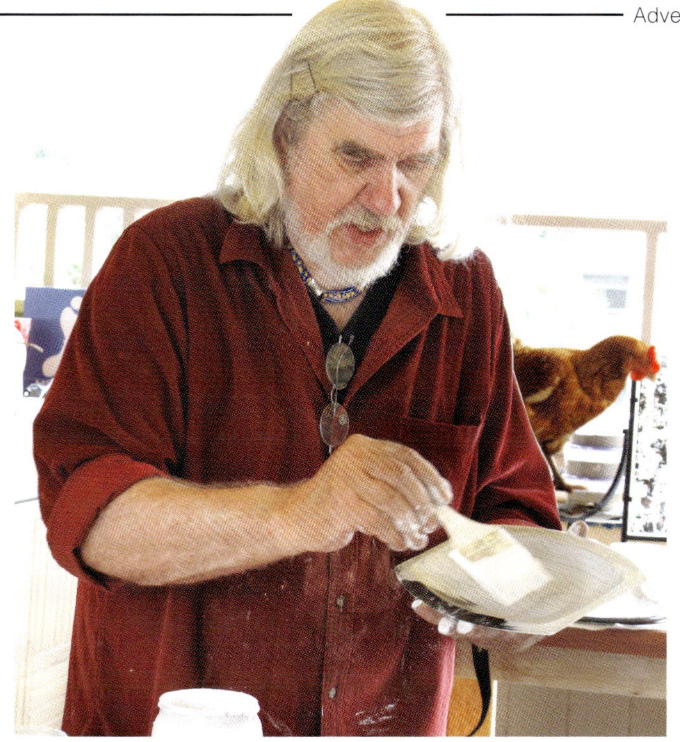

60. *Applying Universal Mold Coat to a stainless steel mold purchased at a thrift store.*

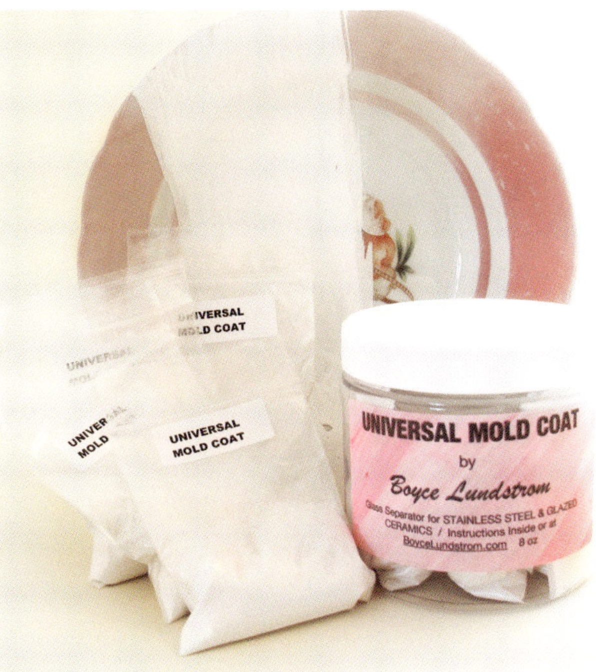

61. *Universal Mold Coat by Boyce Lundstrom available at BoyceLundstrom.com*

prices. This gun will spray thick liquids such as Reactive Dry Enamels and water; you can even spray paint your fence. See photo on previous page of some good spray action.

The uneven spray, the dots and blips and blobs made by cheaper, less conventional sprayers, I believe, add to the Raku Glass sensitivity, character, and mystery.

Finishing the Piece

The "glass sandwich" is now ready for fusing, using the firing program referred to as "Program 1- Debubble". This program has been designed to raise temperatures very slowly during the beginning of the slump—a temperature range between 1050° F and 1150° F for 90 COE glass. NOTE: When firing window glass, move the temperature range to 1100° F to 1175° F.

When the glass has finished the fusing process, check the edges to see that they are smooth before slumping. If not, sand with 'wet or dry' sandpaper. Clean the fused piece.

If you chose a bisque ware slumping mold use a regular shelf primer for a glass separator. If you chose a glazed mold from the local thrift shop or from your cupboard, then use Universal Primer, following the instructions, to coat the mold. (The molds chosen for all of our classes are purchased at second-hand stores.) There is no need to drill any holes in the glazed dish being used for the mold, unless it is over 2 1/2" to 3" deep.

The last step for this project is to place the fused glass piece on the mold in the kiln and fire it, using the "Program 2 – Slump" firing schedule. (See page 26).

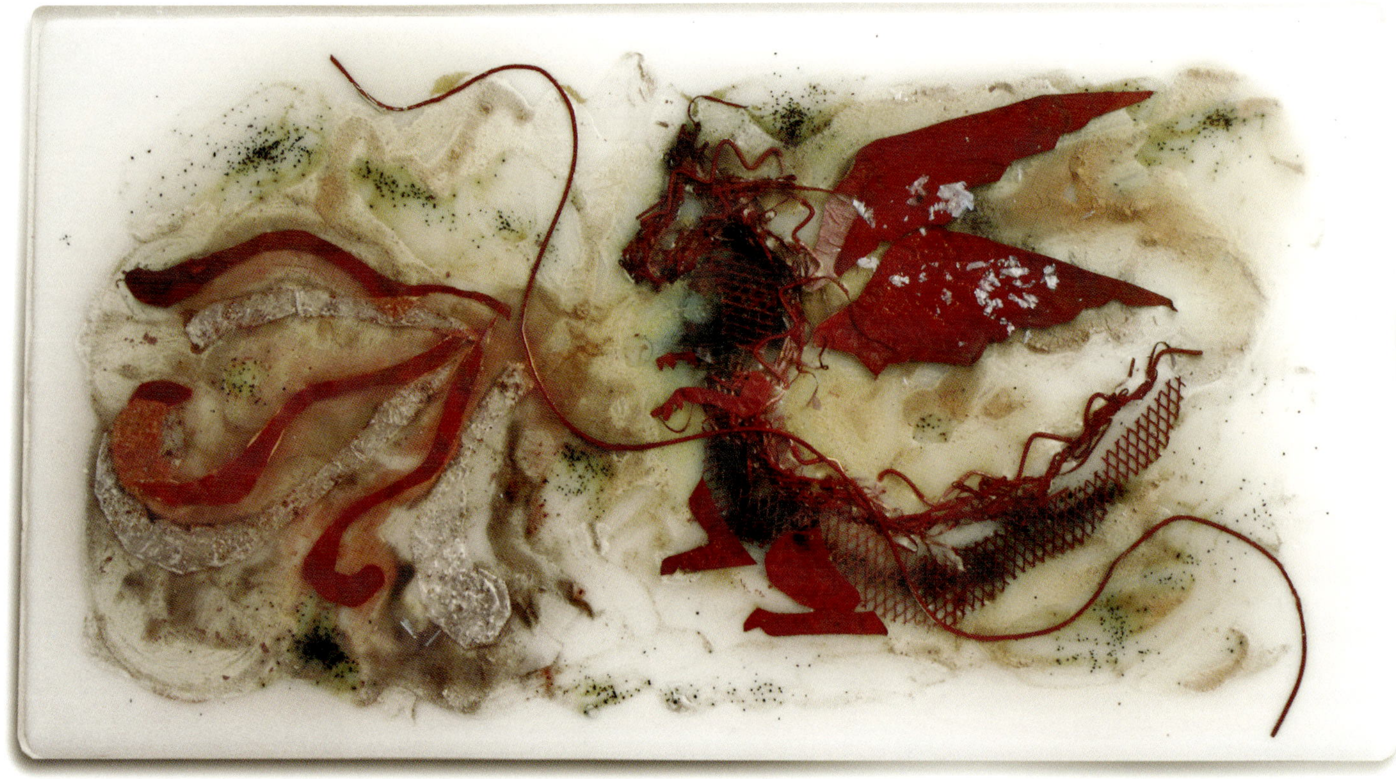

62. *Winged Dragon tile by Dana Taylor, approx 6" X 12".*

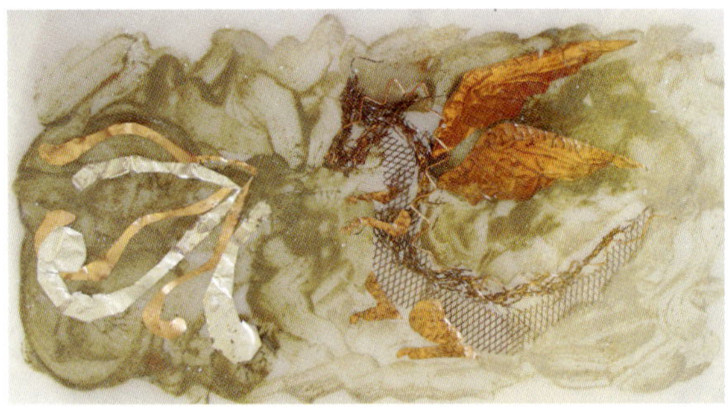

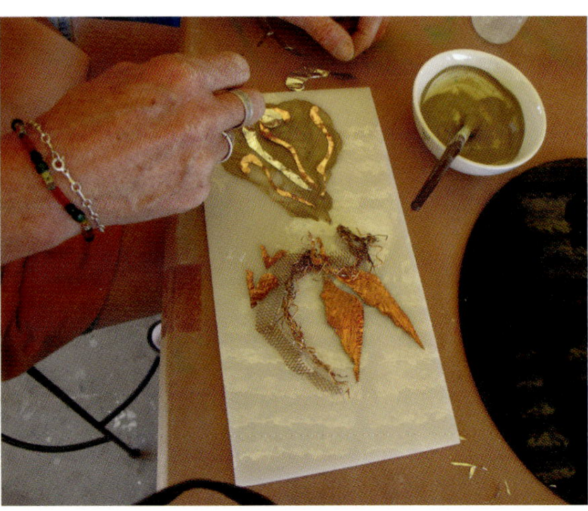

Condiments

The number of materials you can capture between glass layers is daunting. Many can be found in the grocery or hardware store. The rule of thumb is, if you haven't tried it, try it! Here are some of the materials I've experimented with and found to be useful in the development of distinctive colors and textures. Since there is a limit to the number of variables I can include in this booklet, I am listing only a relatively few materials. From the Hardware Store or Home Depot, you can purchase liquid solder, brass shim stock, small copper nails, copper washers, copper rings, copper pipe,

63–64. *The many layers of various metals took time to place, so the background enamel was painted on the glass in small applications as the tile was constructed. The wings were cut from weathered copper (studio scrap). Pieces left out in the open change color.*

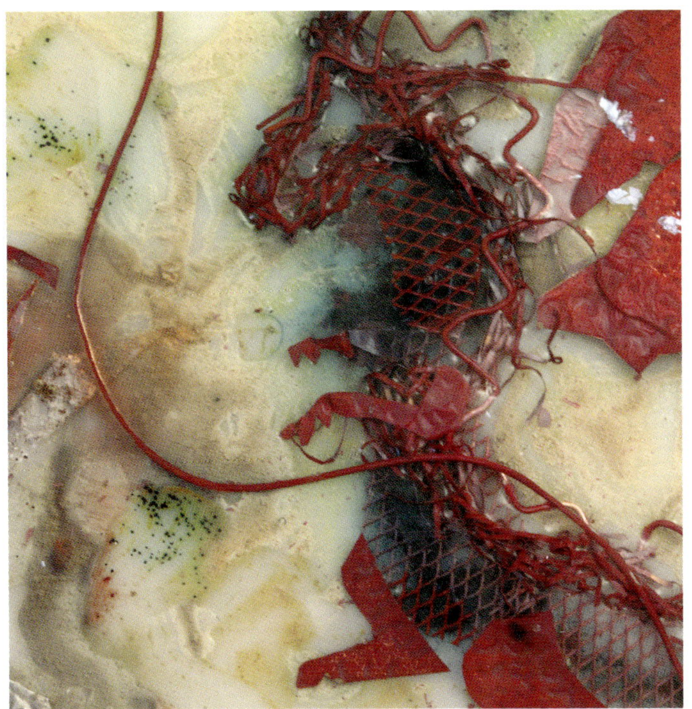

65. *Copper mesh and pieces of copper kitchen scrubber were used for the dragon's body. The 16 gauge copper wire allowed most of the trapped air to dissipate.*

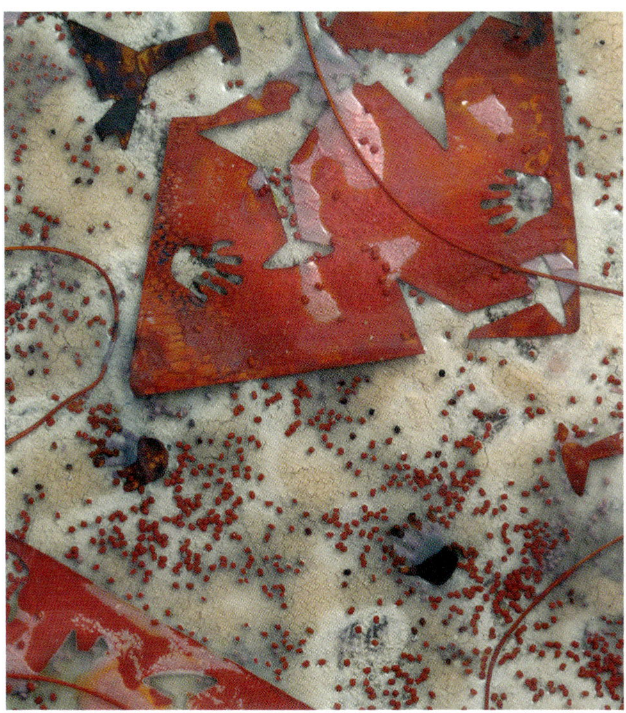

66. *Copper foil was cut with a punch. The hands and martini glass hole punches are available at craft supply stores. Note the large grains of copper are red.*

copper cable, and braided copper wire. In the garden department, you can get bone ash, copper sulfate, iron sulfate, urea, charcoal, and of course a large variety of pots to use as molds.

On your way home, stop by the grocery store and get silver polish that specifically says "Not for Copper", boric acid (used as ant killer), oven cleaner, Epson salt, cream of tartar, sodium borate (i.e. Borax), potassium chloride (a common salt substitute), aluminum foil, and copper scrubbies.

The aluminum foil you purchase in the grocery store is either heavy duty or household regular. Heavy duty is 1.3 mil thick and regular is half that thickness. (Remember, when talking thickness of metals, we refer to the mil. This does not mean millimeter but rather refers to thousandths, .003 equals 3/1000 of an inch.) Aluminum soft-drink cans are 5 mil thick and work well as inclusions in float glass. Often, bubbling caused by the can coating creates a texture of very small bubbles that can't rise to the surface because of the stiffness of the float glass.

Also, I have found that ashes from my fireplace, when washed and water separated, do fantastic things inside the glass. There is also mud from the lagoon, synthetic oil leftover from your last oil change, and charcoal briquettes to create a reduction atmosphere in the kiln. And, I almost forgot, for reduction, putting mothballs in your 'peep hole' is as good as it sounds.

Yahoo Raku!

Program 1: Full Fuse - DeBubble

Ramp (F)	To Temp (F)	Hold, Soak
300º / hr	450º / hr	
500º / hr	1050º / hr	10 min
75º / hr	1175º / hr	20 min
500º / hr	1430º / hr	15 min
Full (off)	920º	15 min
50º / hr	870º	30 min

Program 2: Slump

Ramp (F)	To Temp (F)	Hold, Soak
300º / hr	500º	NO
500º	1250º	5 min
Full (off)	920º	15 min
50º / hr	870º	30 min
off		

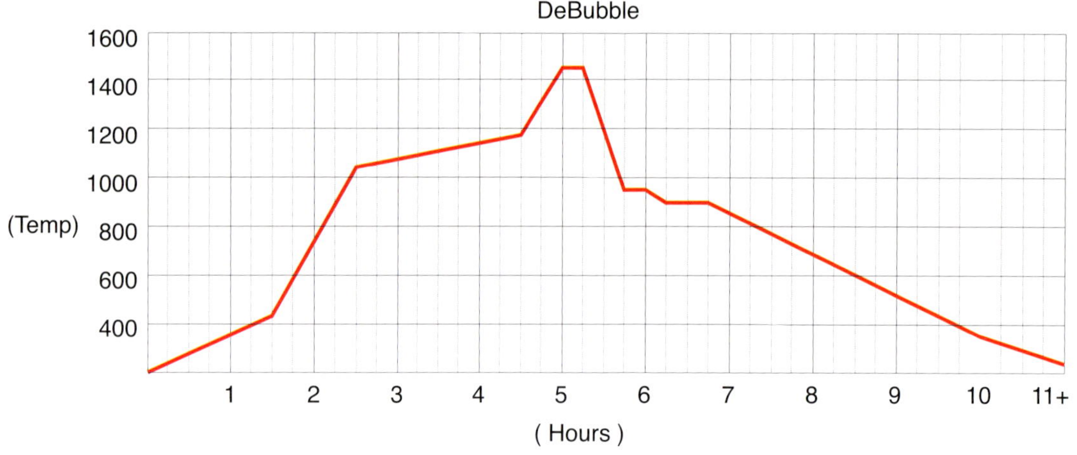

Program 3

Refine, Refuse or Add a Layer of Glass

Ramp (F)	To Temp (F)	Hold, Soak
200º / hr	450º / hr	
400º / hr	1050º / hr	10 min
75º / hr	1175º / hr	20 min
500º / hr	1440º / hr	15 min
Full (off)	920º	15 min
50º / hr	870º	30 min

Program 4

Float Glass Fuse: Apx. 100° above other Programs

Ramp (F)	To Temp (F)	Hold, Soak
300º / hr	500º	NO
500º	1150º	15 min
75º / hr	1250º	30 min
500º /hr	1550º	10 min
Full (off)	1020º	15 min
50º / hr	970º	30 min

Fire float glass with 'tin' side out.

Firing

The firing schedules given above are general outlines for Wissmach 90 and should be changed to suit your kiln. The final temperature and the amount of time held are usually changed most often. My Firebox 110 will fuse with rounded edges at 20° F before my BonnyGlo Fiber 110 volt kiln.

Bubbles

There are bubbles formed in just about all pieces when using Reactive Dry Enamels and metal inclusions. To keep the bubbles small, keep your full fuse temperature as low as possible. I fire to 1430° F for most pieces and hold for 20 minutes. The trapped air does not expand as much at this lower fusing temperature so the bubbles stay smaller.

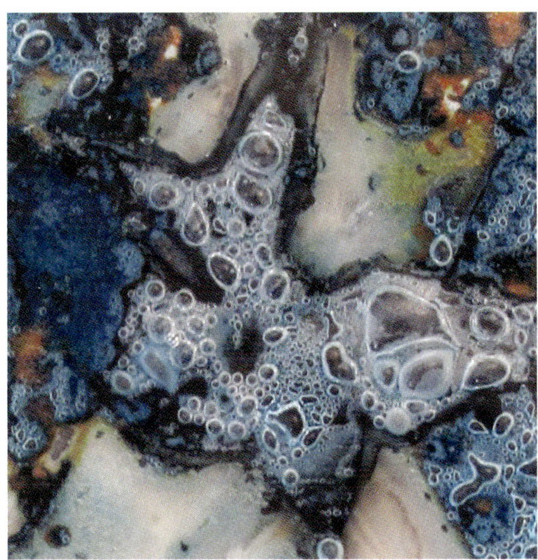

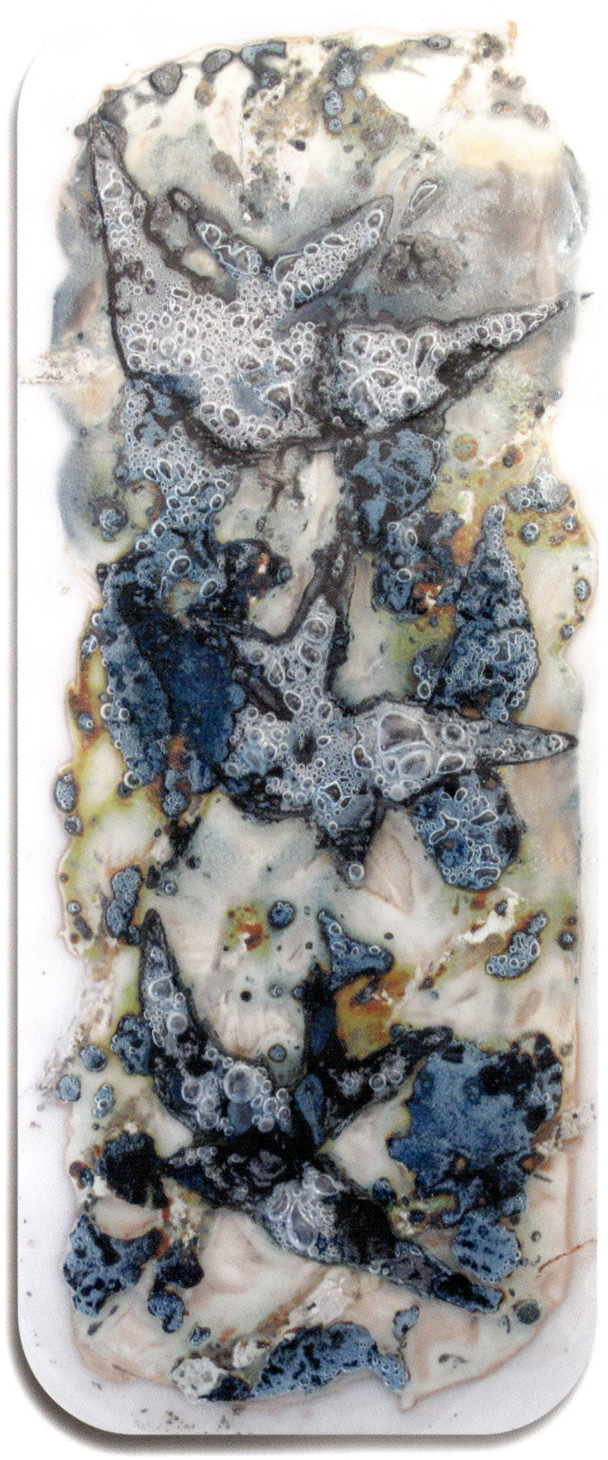

Inspiration

I would write a Haiku to help describe my feelings for this new glass process, if there was not an American form of poetry more suitable for English language expression. So, here is my Cinquain, with its two, four, six, eight, two, cadence.

RAKU
Oil slick patterns
Fired between two glasses
The colors uplift my spirit
Yahoo

Glass is a remarkably versatile and exciting material – tempered, drilled, etched, blown, painted, spun into cloth, stretched like taffy, made viscous with heat, polished hot or cold, transparent, iridescent, opalescent, and opaque. Without glass, what would we have used for microscopes or eyeglasses?

Bluebirds in a Bubble by Dana Taylor, 6.5" X 12". The cobalt carbonate color addition created many small bubbles and 1 big bubble making this piece only connected at the edges.

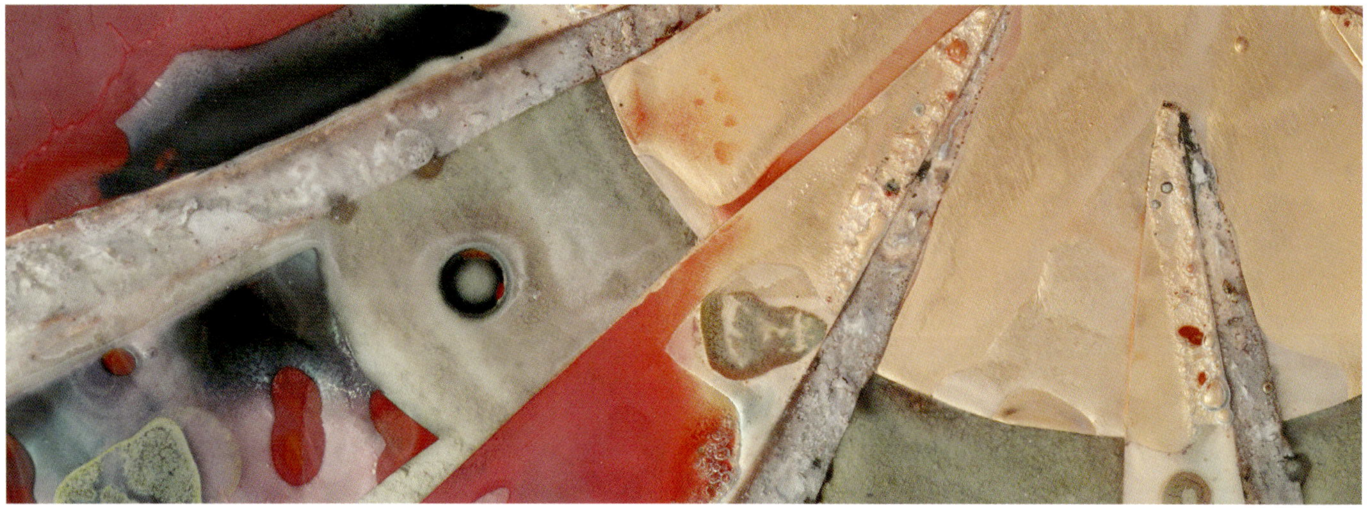

67. *Close-up of finished piece using geometric design. Copper triangles with aluminum shadows.*

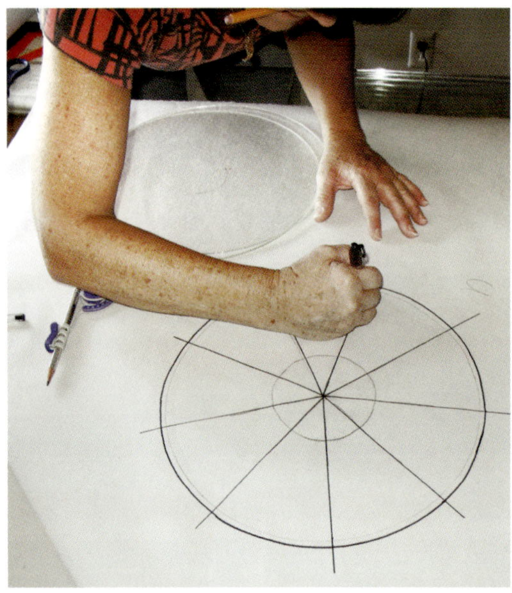

68. *Creating a geometric template.*

Geometric Design Method

In Book One, Kiln Fired Glass with Copper & Metal Inclusions, I described the process of embossing copper by preparing a three-dimensional design with found objects and running over them with a car to press the design into copper. Simply put, “Auto Embossing”.

Geometric designs are elements of classical art and classical thought. The design method used in this lesson we call concentric design placement. We place cut-out metal elements within a geometric template. This is done on a glass blank on top of a reactive enamel. The chemical reaction will outline the metal form with a contrasting color. These colors will then create new shapes. This is good, this is what we want; we are creating a source of inspiration.

Once we leave the three-dimensional world of cutting shapes out of copper or aluminum foil and lay our metal on a one-dimensional plane, we enter the world of abstract composition. I have provided a pullout template to aid in your design. Any shape having a common center is considered concentric design. By taking away the realism, you can concentrate on the visual balance of color and shape.

69. *Three geometric templates showing the varieties of design that can be made by dividing any shape into sections. (Opposite Page)*

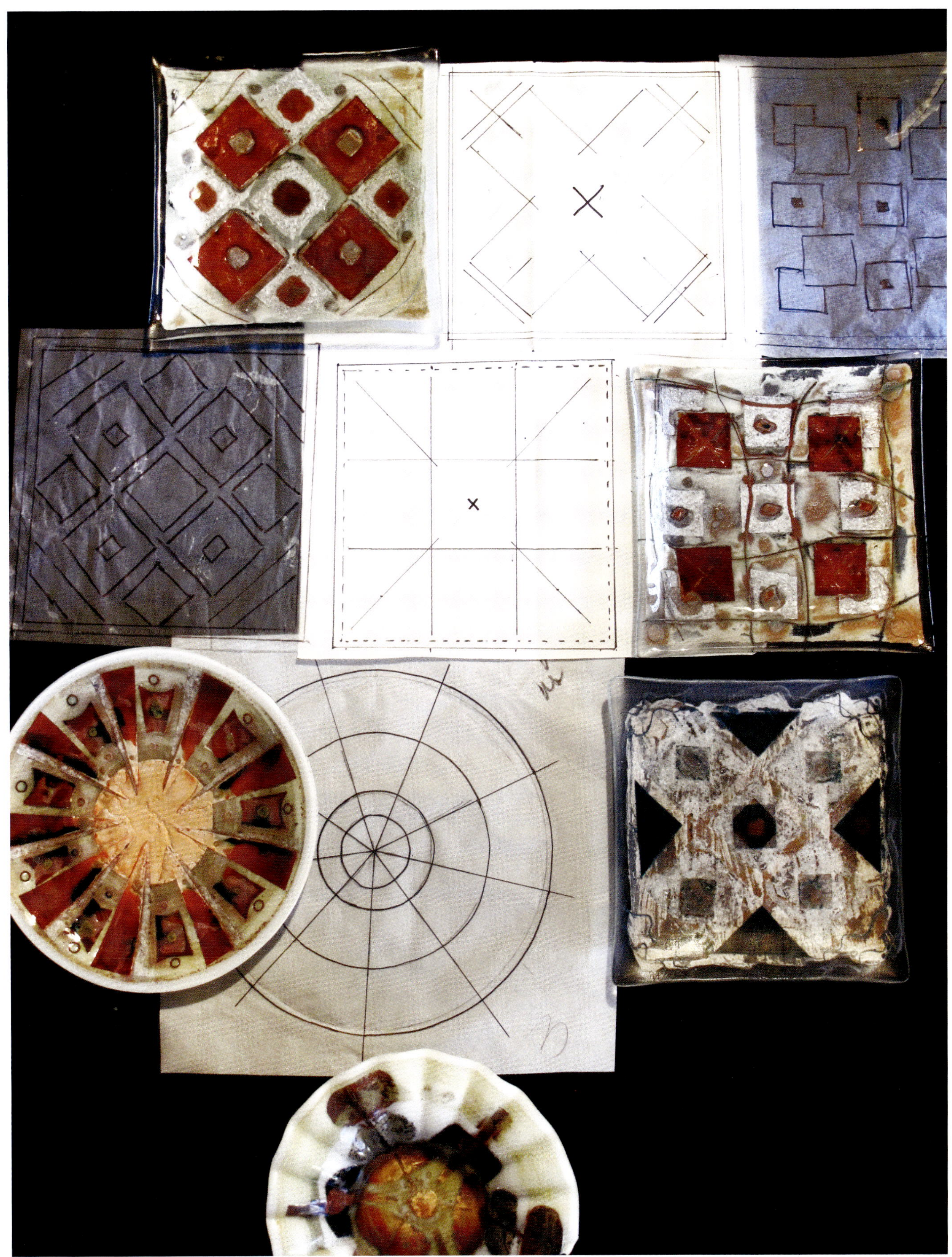

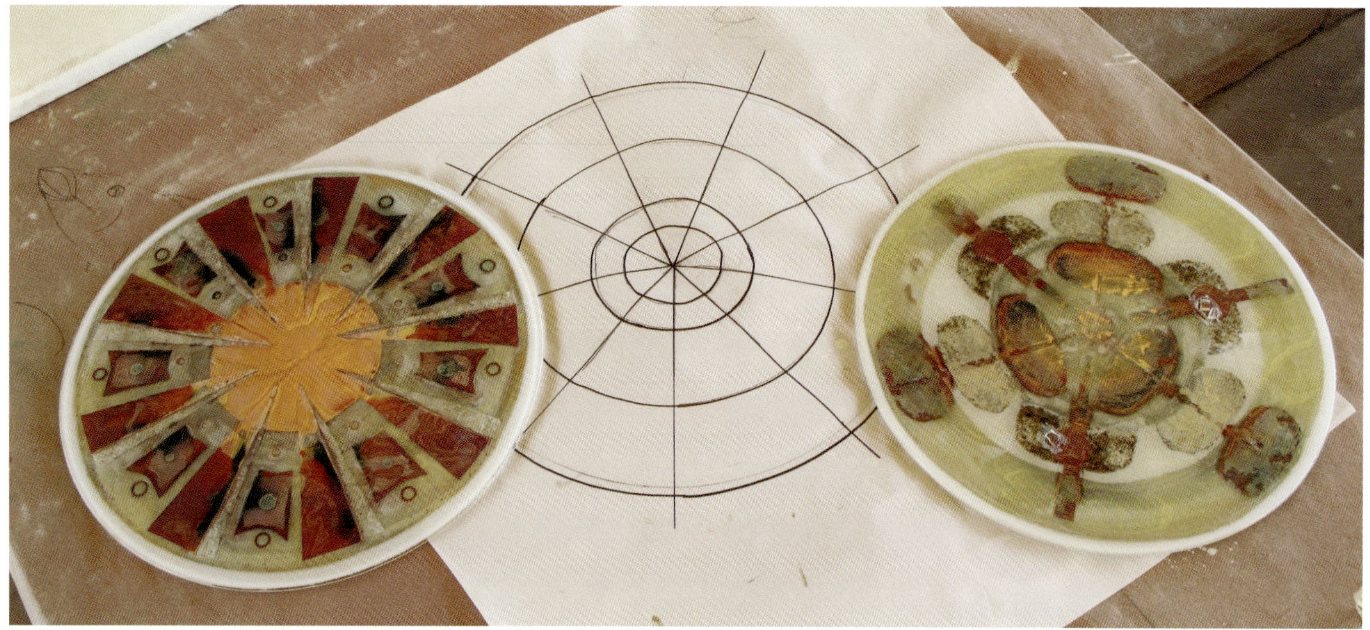

70. *Both plates were designed on the same template. The first was nine triangles, the second is three.*

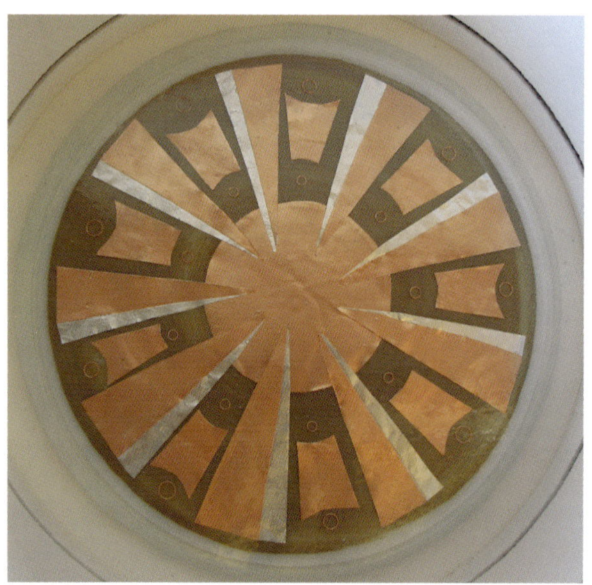

71. *Lay-up of cut copper pieces on Reactive Dry Enamel before firing. This design was cut and assembled in about 15 minutes.*

In this first project, left in photo #70, we started with 12 1/4" white and clear circle glass blanks so we could make the maximum size to fit on our 13" kiln shelf.

Following the circle design in the foldout, we cut copper and aluminum elements and arranged them on the template, being careful to leave a 1/4" edge all around for glass to properly seal.

We painted the white blank with Green Earth Reactive Dry Enamel, which was mixed 1/2 hour earlier to a medium thickness. When we added the copper and aluminum cutouts some wet Green Earth came over the edges, adding smudges to the copper foil. Rings were added to the top of the cutouts. Since the circle and triangles were pre-cut, the assembly time was only about five minutes.

The next step was to carefully place the clear blank over the piece, making sure all the edges were evenly aligned. This was then allowed to sit for 2 1/2 hours to let the metal react to the chemicals in the mud.

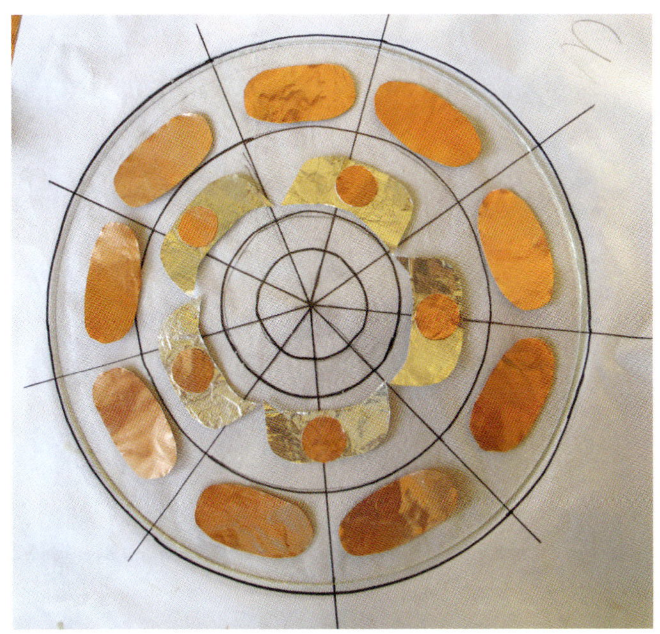

72. *"Potato" shaped copper pieces in an experimental layout not executed.*

73. *Final layout with previous shapes showing experimental purple on aluminum and Reactive Dry Enamel painted on clear blank before placing on top of design.*

The piece was then fired using the "DeBubble" Kiln Schedule #1.

The same design concept and template were used for the second project, on right in photo #70, but with unique results. "Potato" shaped copper cutouts were originally arranged using the entire template. However, we used fewer of the sections, creating a design very different from the first.

These elements were placed on a white glass blank and secured using a small dot of glue. Then the clear blank was brushed with Green Earth Reactive Dry Enamel while it was turning on a 'lazy susan.'

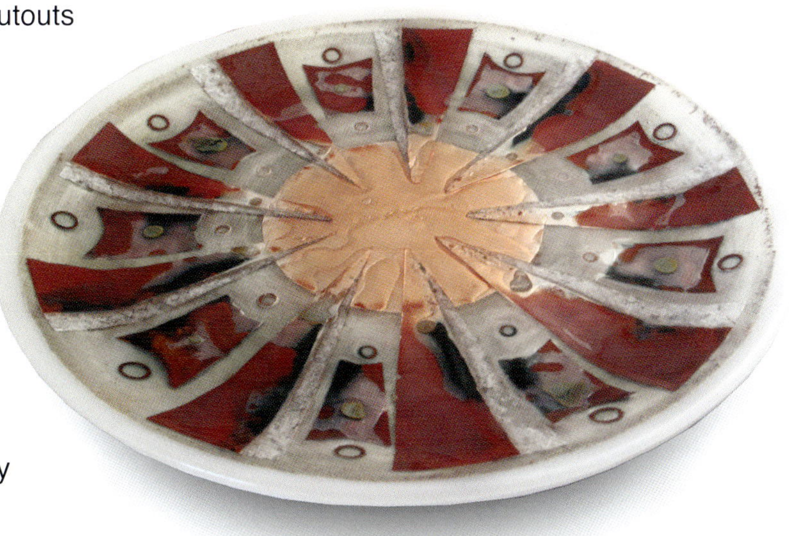

74. *Finished plate by Donna, a seamstress who's never done glass before, using templates in this book.*

The painted clear blank was carefully placed on the white glass, paint side down, and allowed to sit for two hours to let the mud react with the metal. We then fired it using the "DeBubble" Schedule #1.

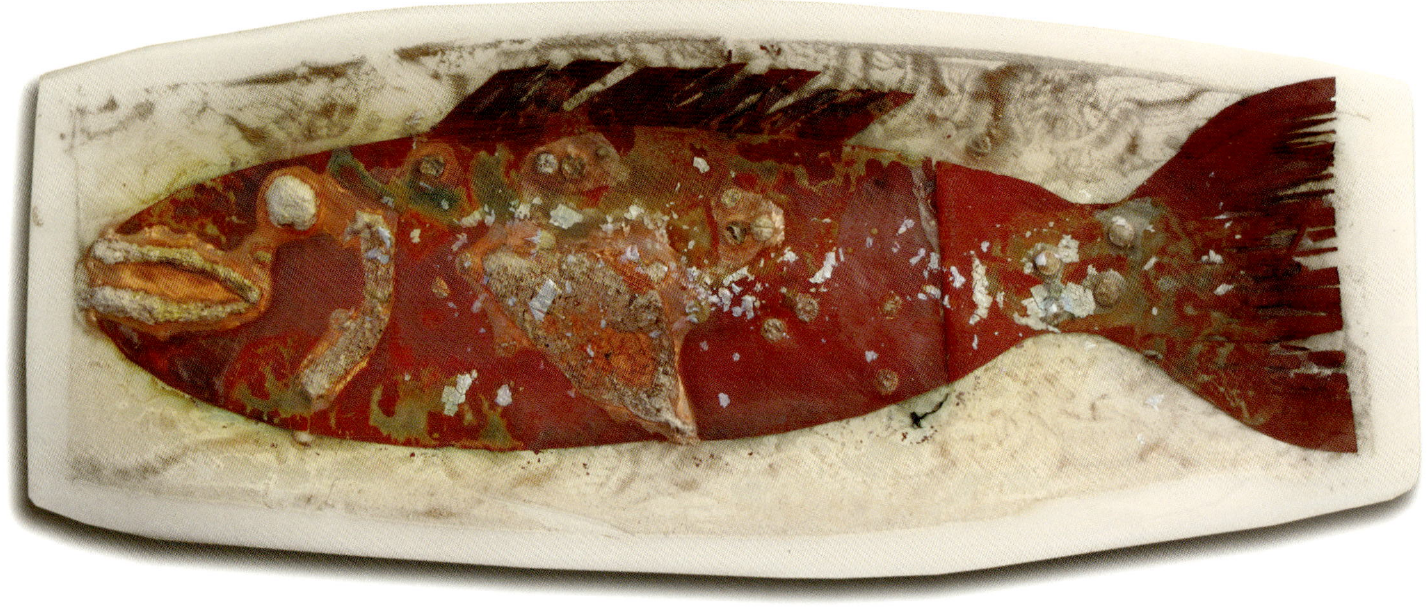

75. *Marc's fish platter using aluminum 'punch-cut' designs and dichroic sprinkles for texture on copper, placed on Reactive Dry Enamel.*

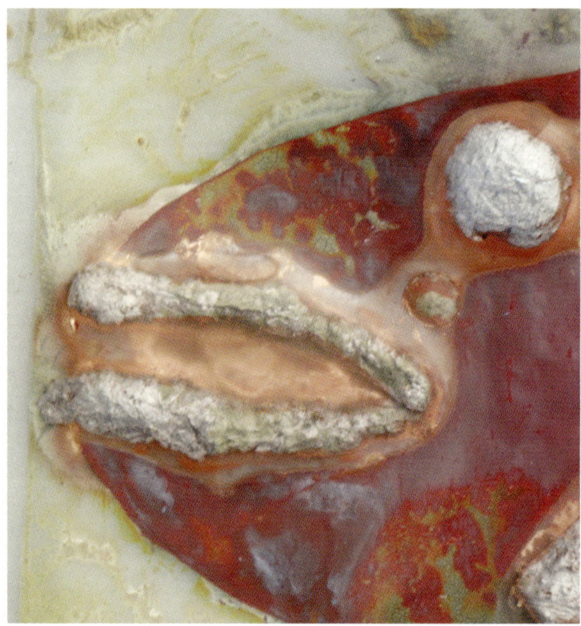

76. *Close-up showing dimensional "rolled" aluminum lips, eyes and gills. Smudges of reactive enamel on copper fish create texture.*

of color and shape.

Fusing Discussion

The use of volume (thickness) to control the shape and size of the finished, fully fused glass blank is covered very well in Glass Fusing Book 1 by Boyce Lundstrom, and the other four available books that explain the basic fusing process. What should be realized when fusing a large metal inclusion of copper between two 1/8" layers of glass is that the metal does not chemically bond with the glass, therefore only the edges of the fused blank are holding the piece together. Some mechanical bond does exist between the layers of glass and metal, but this bond does not affect the need of the glass to maintain the necessary 1/4" thickness that is required for the glass

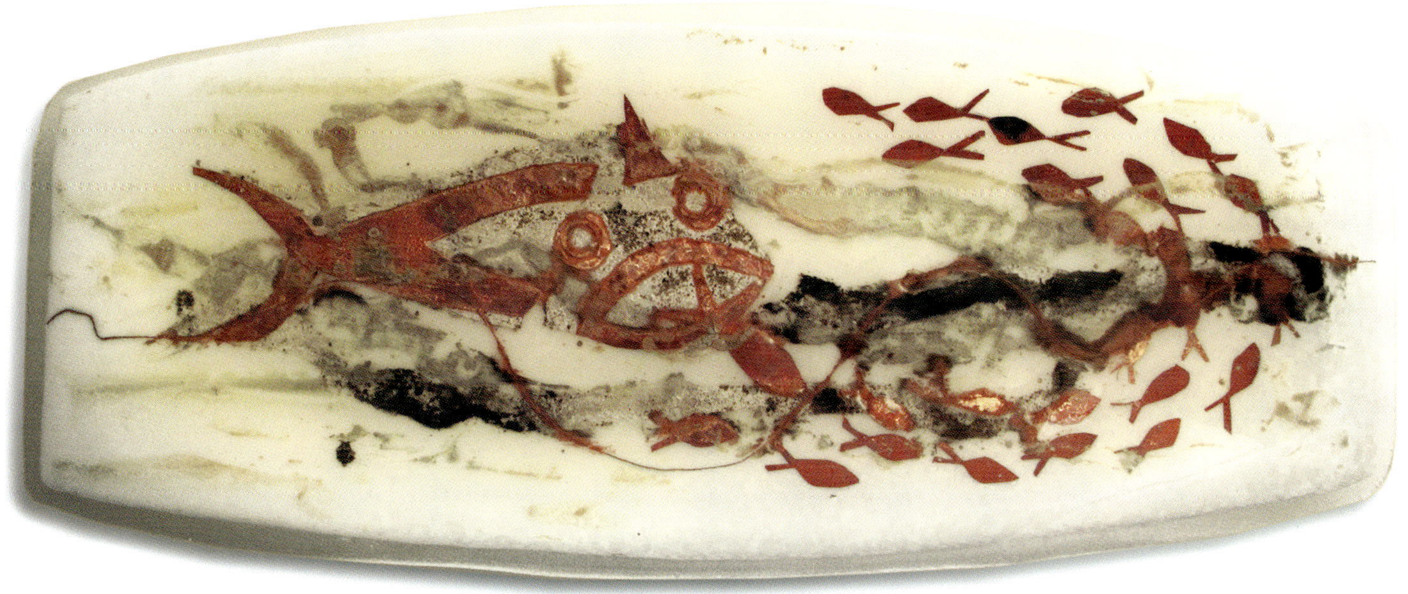

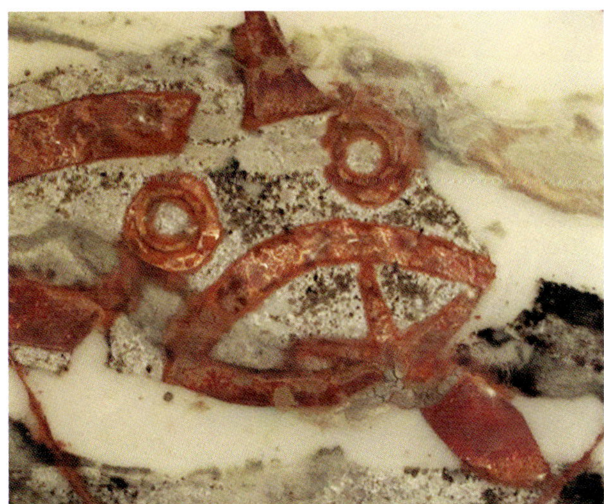

77. *Fish Platter #2 "Grouper Chases School of Herring". Small pieces of scrap of copper, aluminum and wire were used. Enamel applied, as cutouts were placed on bottom blank.*

to flow rather than contract. What this means is that if a 1/8" piece of glass is not contiguous, the separate pieces will fuse on the edges where there are two 1/8" layers and no metal. However, they may separate on the surface where there is a butt joint. If a piece is over-fired, a small crack may open in the top piece of glass. All glass, when taken to full fuse temperatures, "wants to be" 1/4" (or more) thick. The pictures on these pages show some of the effects that are created by glass thickness.

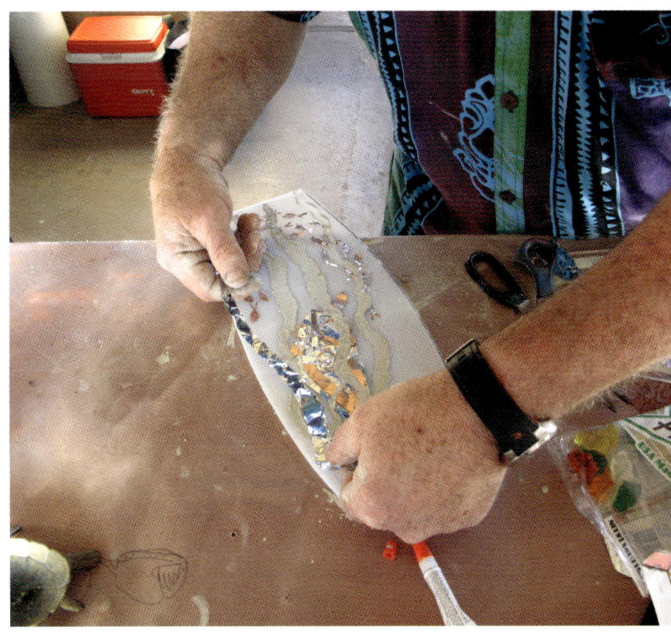

78. *Marc, high on 'gummie bears', assembling above piece.*

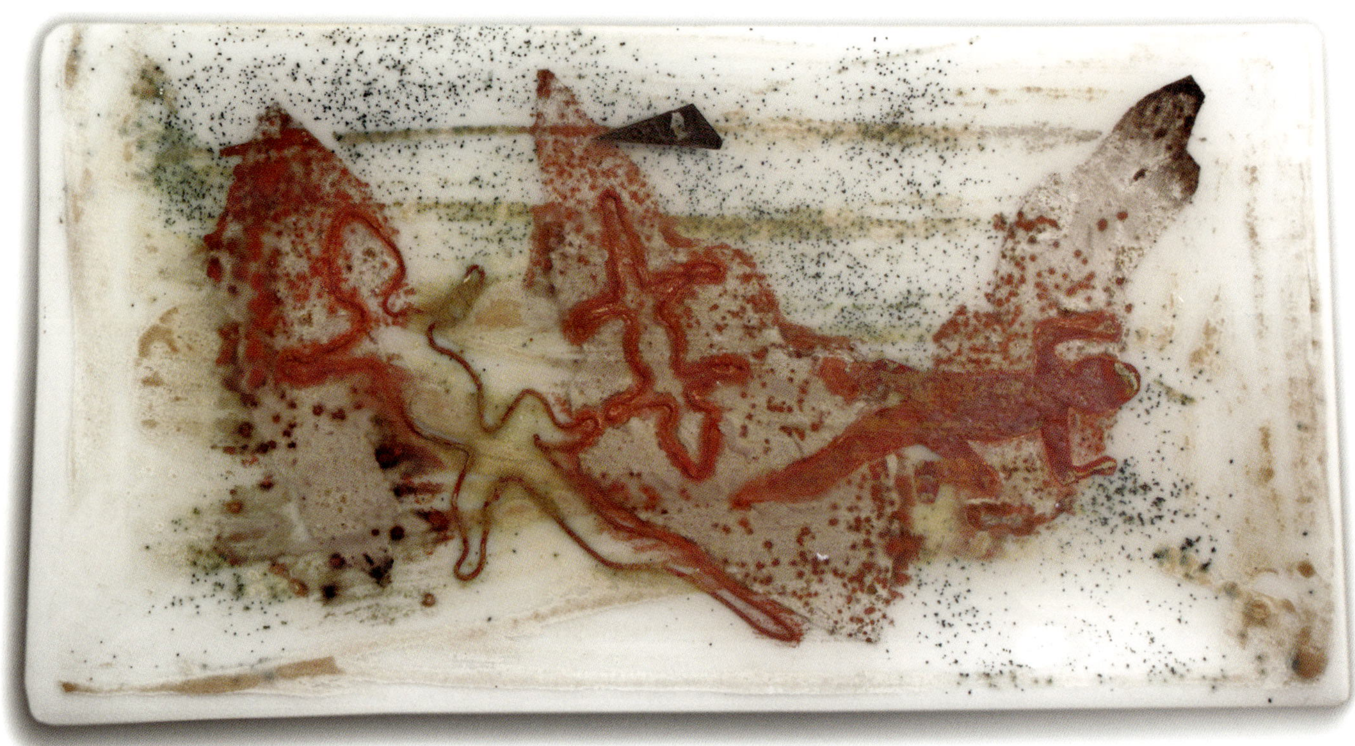

79. *Center lizard bent from 22-gauge wire was oxidized at 700° F and placed over aluminum. Using aluminum under the copper lizards acted as a reducing flux creating a red copper halo.*

Flux and Refractory

Reactive Dry enamel is applied wet. When on top of a glass surface it does not flux. It is a refractory or high temperature material. Basically a flux lowers the melting point of any material it is mixed with or applied over.

I promote the use of lead in my new craft materials list as a basic flux. It has, for me, to be introduced as a way of refuting the bad rap lead has been given by business and government. Lead frits, or lead-containing glasses, will not jump out of a bag and go in your nose or into your mouth and make you stupid. Just remember to wash your hands. I think lead-containing glasses are essential and add ease of working and cure many of the inconsistencies,

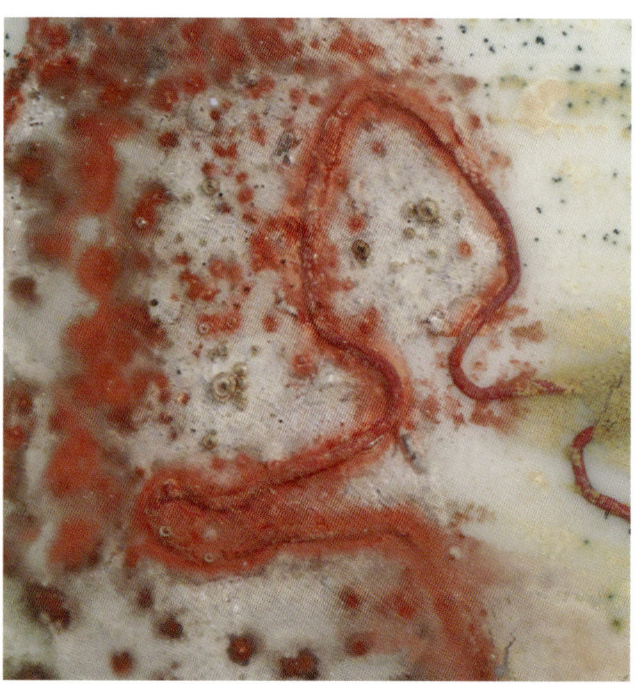

80. *Close-up of sushi plate in photo #79 showing copper granules; red over aluminum and green when on reactive enamel.*

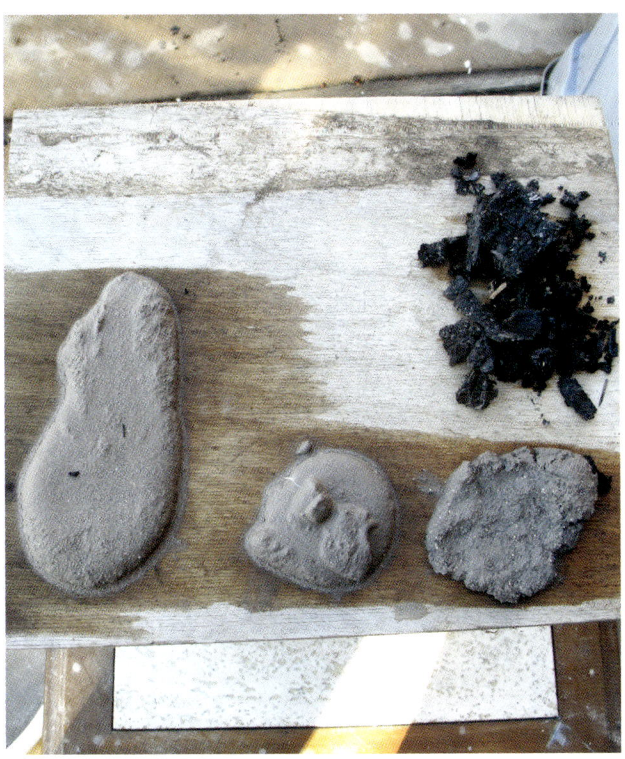

81. *Samples of three different layers of ash, spooned onto wood to dry.*

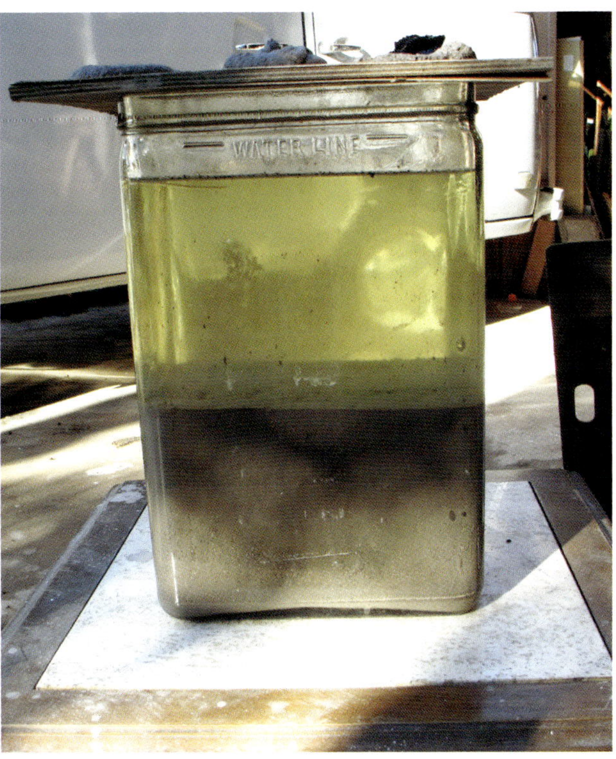

82. *Fireplace ash being water-washed and separated, then strained into glass container. As the ash settles, the heavy particles sink first, then the silt particles last. After settling, the water is siphoned off the top, and the ash is air-dried for three or four days.*

mistakes or flaws craftsmen acquire in their work because nothing works like lead frit. I use Ferro # 3470. I use this flux to mix with silt from the lagoon, different colors of clay I find in road-cut excavation, as well as my fireplace ash, and in fine garden clay. If you live near a dry lakebed or any other recognizable formation, test the soil, clay or silt and mix it with water-separated fireplace ash. This will give you a start on creating your own dry enamel.

Spray A, a material I invented in 1981, is an overglaze containing lead. Its purpose is to keep opal from devitrifying. It also keeps the surface of all float glass from devitrifying. Spray A was and is the industry standard. This material, which contains lead, is safe to use. Just clean your hands and your work areas on a regular basis.

Create a Personal Recipe for Dry Enamel

A large variety of materials around your home will work.

One part fine fireplace ash
One part Gertsley-Borate or Ferro Flux #3470
One part fine clay from your area
(sticky blue, black or brown is best)
A pinch of copper oxide or other metal oxide
2 pinches of baking soda
Salt to taste :)

Studio Learning

I have purposely broken pieces of glass, or sawn fused pieces apart with a diamond saw, to determine how different metals interface with glass when fused together at over 1400° F. I've discovered that the inclusions we put inside the glass do not, for the most part, become part of the glass or form a chemical bond. The inclusions are captured within the glass envelope, held together by the fusing of the glass edges.

My studio is often littered with experimental fusings, some of which I judge to be worth a second firing. I am always looking at what doesn't work, or what seems to work the way I want it to. I often embrace the accidents, the fortuitous glitches, the bubbles and failures that sometimes disappoint, but that also inspire. I have tried cutting odd fusings into mosaic tiles. When I do this, of course, approximately 1/3 of the cut tiles separate at the metal-glass interface. But I re-fuse the mosaic pieces at a temperature of 1520° F, 100° F hotter than the initial firing, after placing a larger piece of clear glass to cover the cut mosaic piece. The clear glass flows around the edges, encapsulating the exposed copper edge. This particular mosaic, as shown in photos #84 & 85, was a great inspiration to the jewelry designers.

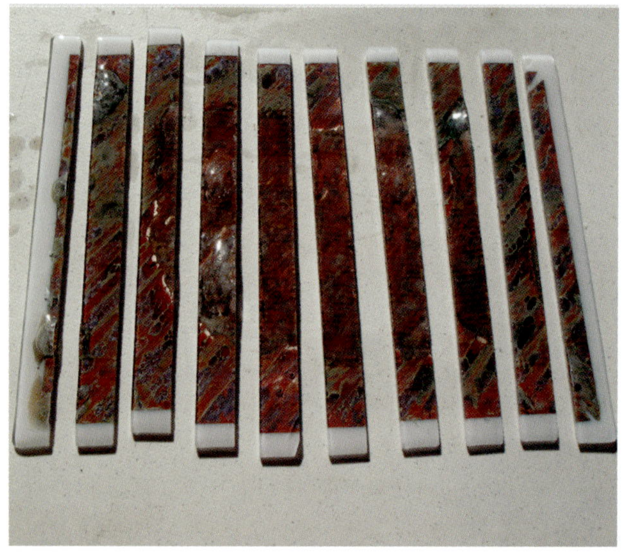

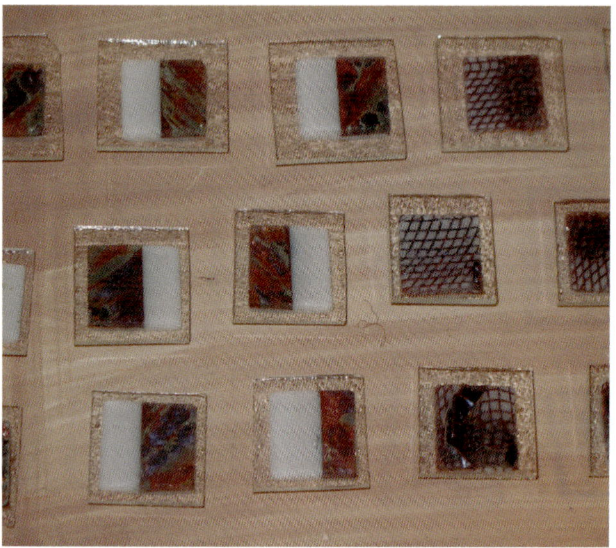

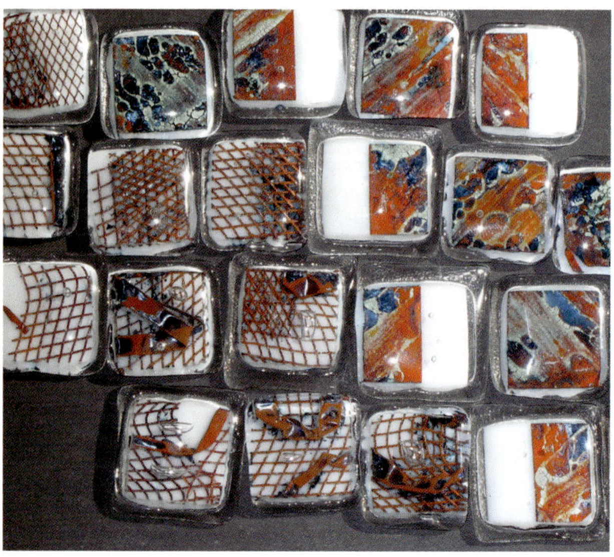

83. *Strips cut from fused tile with popped bubbles.*

84. *Cut pieces with larger clear blank on top, creating 3rd layer.*

85. *Fused mosaics held together with clear glass folded over exposed edges.*

Kiln Choice

In this book, I have limited my exploration to 110-volt kilns. Eight kiln manufacturers make a seven-sided insulated brick kiln that usually comes with a 13" round shelf. Since these small craft kilns represent roughly 75% of the kilns used by crafts people today, I am leaving the construction of larger pieces out of this booklet. But I have experimented with larger pieces in my Skutt 28" kiln, because I'm compelled to see copper and aluminum fused with glass in a larger format. One thing I can say, many of the rules change as far as color, bubbles, out-gassing, and slumping characteristics the larger the work becomes. I will try and tackle this information in another book but I am sure many will have wonderful adventures as they continue to climb the size ladder.

The architectural potential for Raku glass should be looked at closely for those inclined to work very large. The low cost per square foot of large work is worth considering, as well as the reduction in preparation time. Wissmach glass can provide 32" X 64" sheets of clear 90 COE in any thickness. Two layers of 5 mil Wissmach would be very architectural. Think Big.

The fusing kiln or ceramic kiln you have available will limit only the size of your project. For this book all of the projects are designed for the Skutt Hot Start or the 14"x14" FireBox kilns. Of course, any kiln of similar size may be used efficiently.

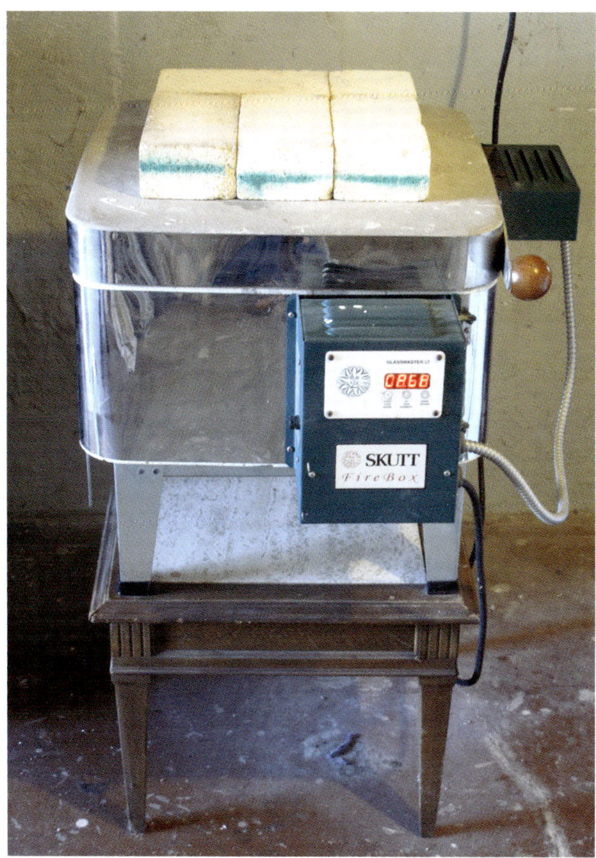

86. *Skutt Firebox, the workhorse for this book, fires full fused and slumps for less than $1 in electricity (with bricks on top).*

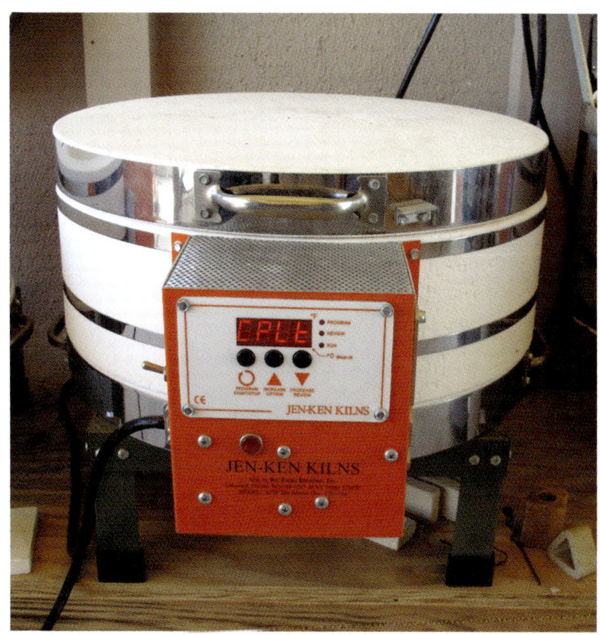

87. *JenKen 'Bonnie Glo', fiber kiln. Fires fast, cools fast, light enough to take on vacation – 28 lbs. My Raku dream.*

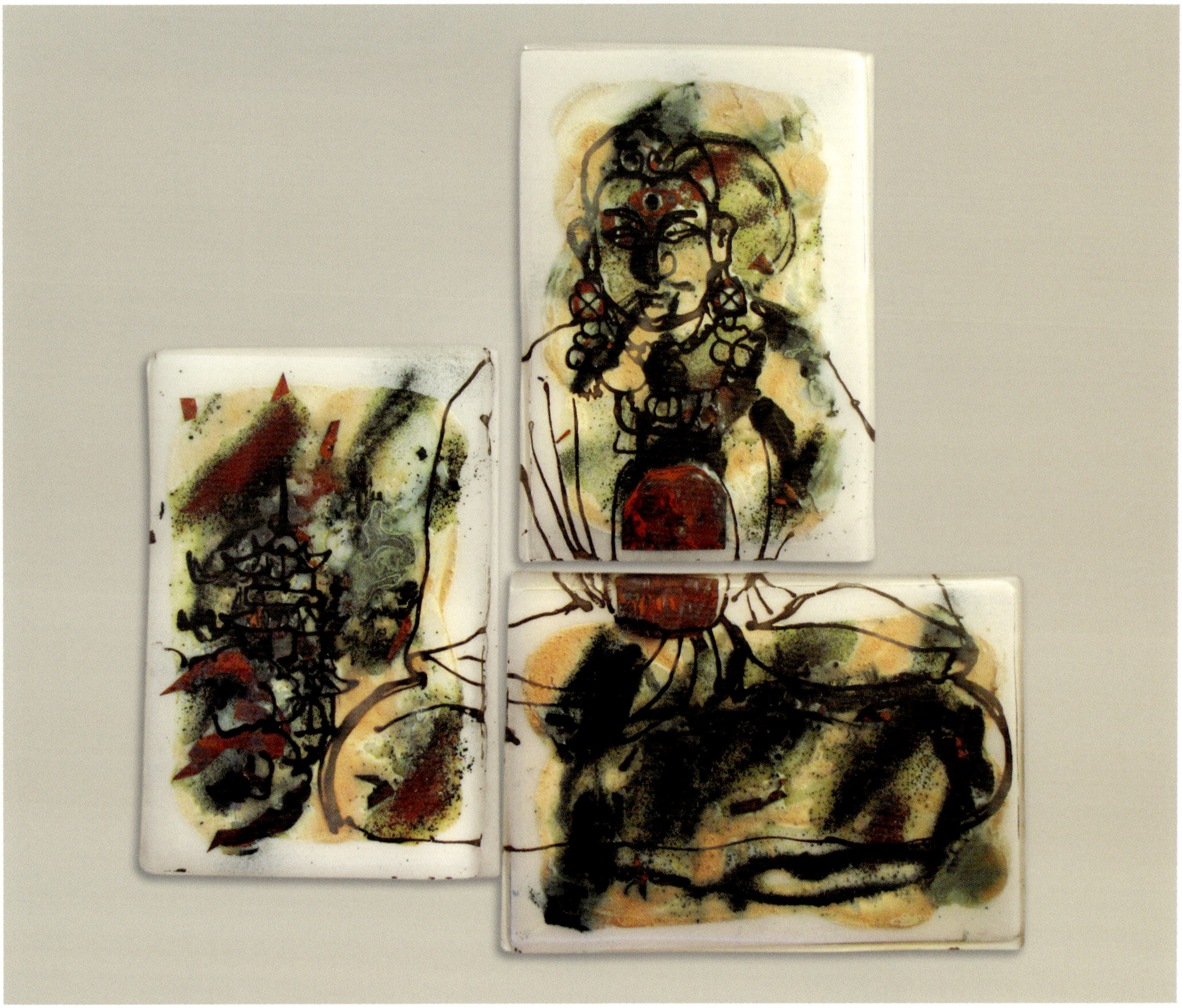

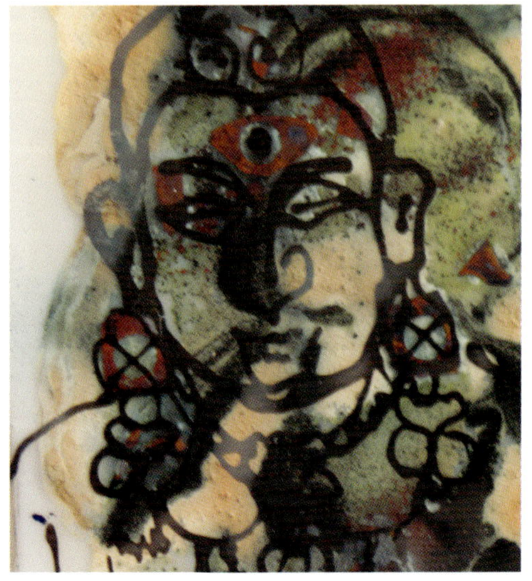

Conclusion

Many may say I have great audacity in calling or referring to a glass process as "Raku Glass." We all know Paul Soldner called Raku a spiritual clay process. The potters who purchase this booklet may need to vent, so please contact me at BoyceLundstrom.com. I think that over time, these glass processes will approach the freedom of Raku.

88. *Triptych by Dana Taylor. One of many quick studies taken from her design book. Design and construction time 30 minutes.*

89. *Close-up of Buddha head.*

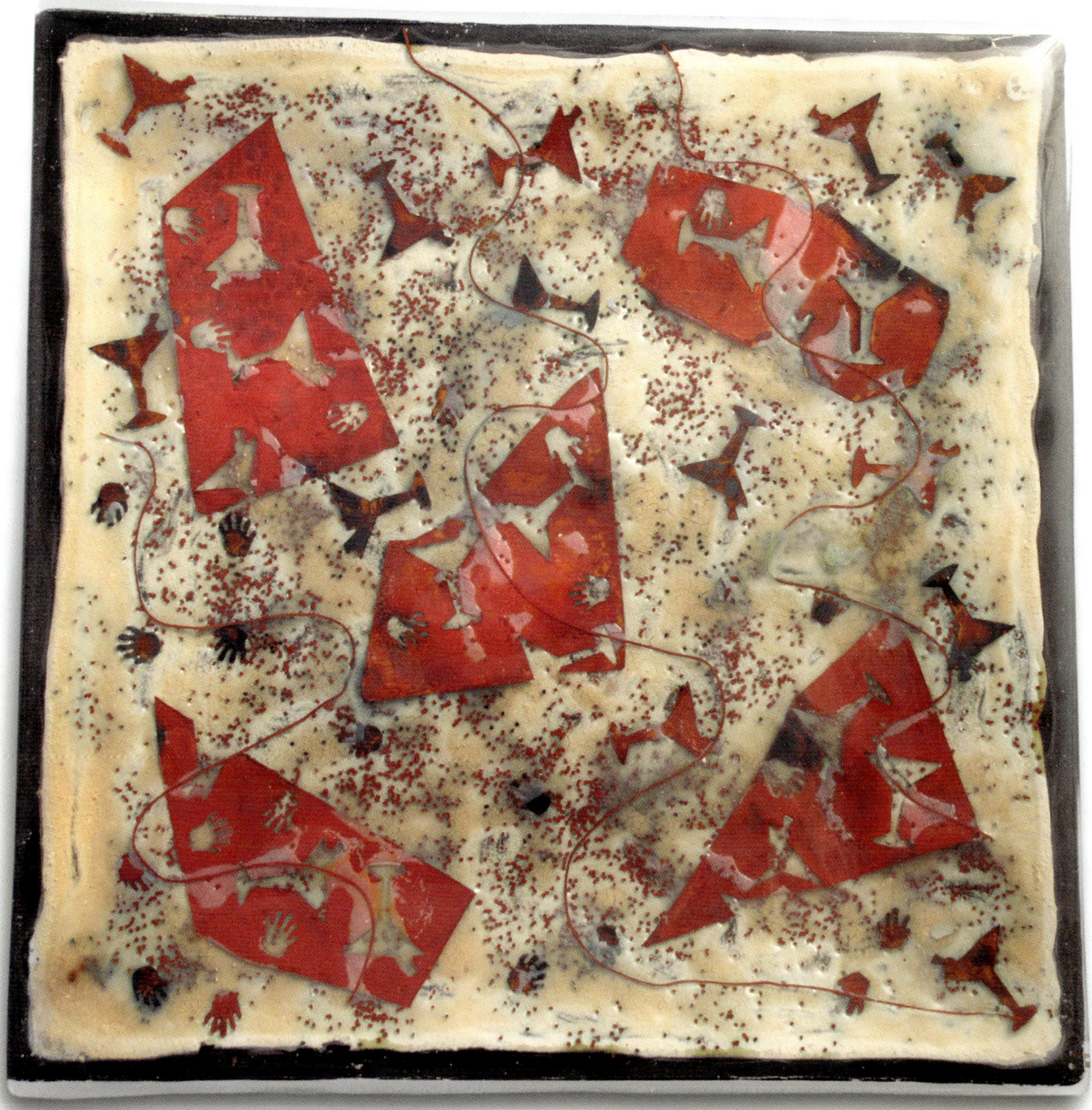

90. *9" X 9" dish "Hand Me A Martini" by Dana Taylor*

Dana Taylor has been my studio assistant for more than ten years. Her work is always exploratory because her job is to work with my new materials. I have dedicated this gallery to Dana Taylor because her innovation and attention to detail need to be seen up close.

With Love,
Boyce

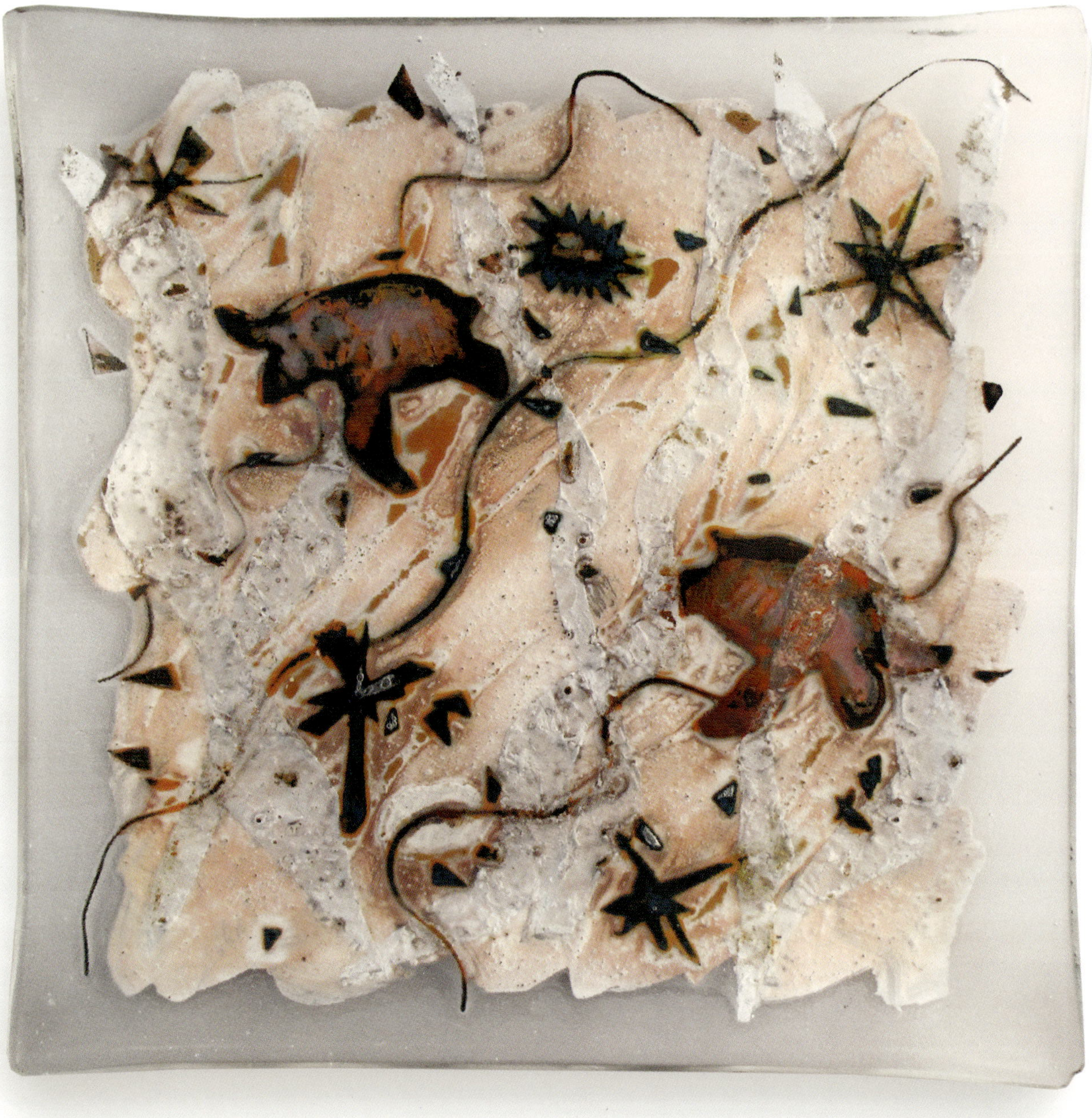

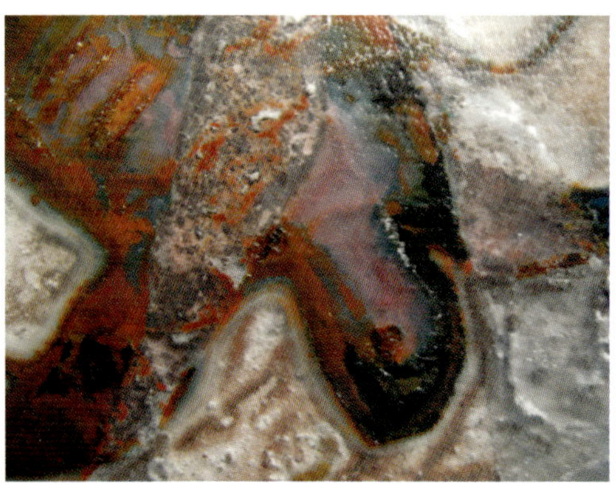

91. *Floating Turtles 10"x10" dish.*

Brown & Green Reactive Dry Enamel applied thick and thin with a brush on clear glass with copper cutouts and wire 'waves' to allow out-gassing. Single strength aluminum foil was applied for 'seaweed' texture. Close-up shows aluminum foil over pen-embossed turtle creating depth of field.

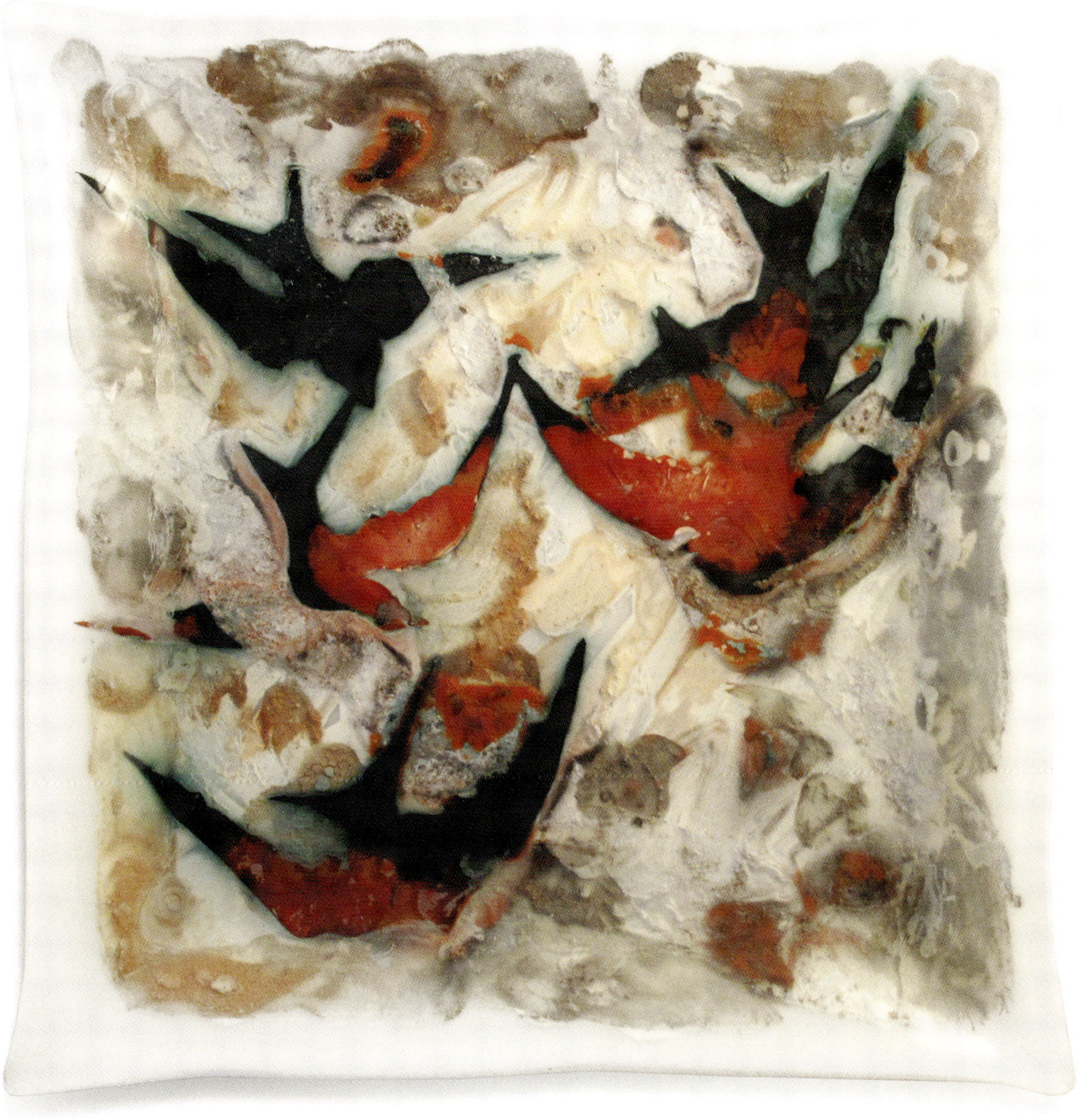

92. *Capistrano Swallows 10"x10" dish.*

Swallows cut from copper scraps placed on hand painted Green Earth and Brown & Green Reactive Dry Enamels. Ribbons of aluminum foil add texture under and on top of birds. Copper scraps are previously handled and weathered. Chemical contaminants on the copper cause color changes.

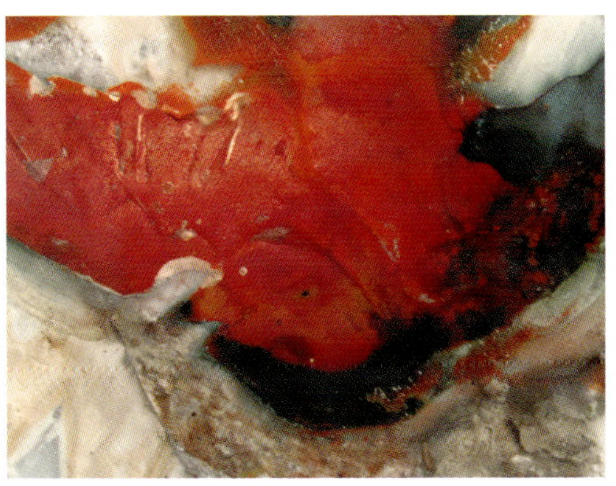

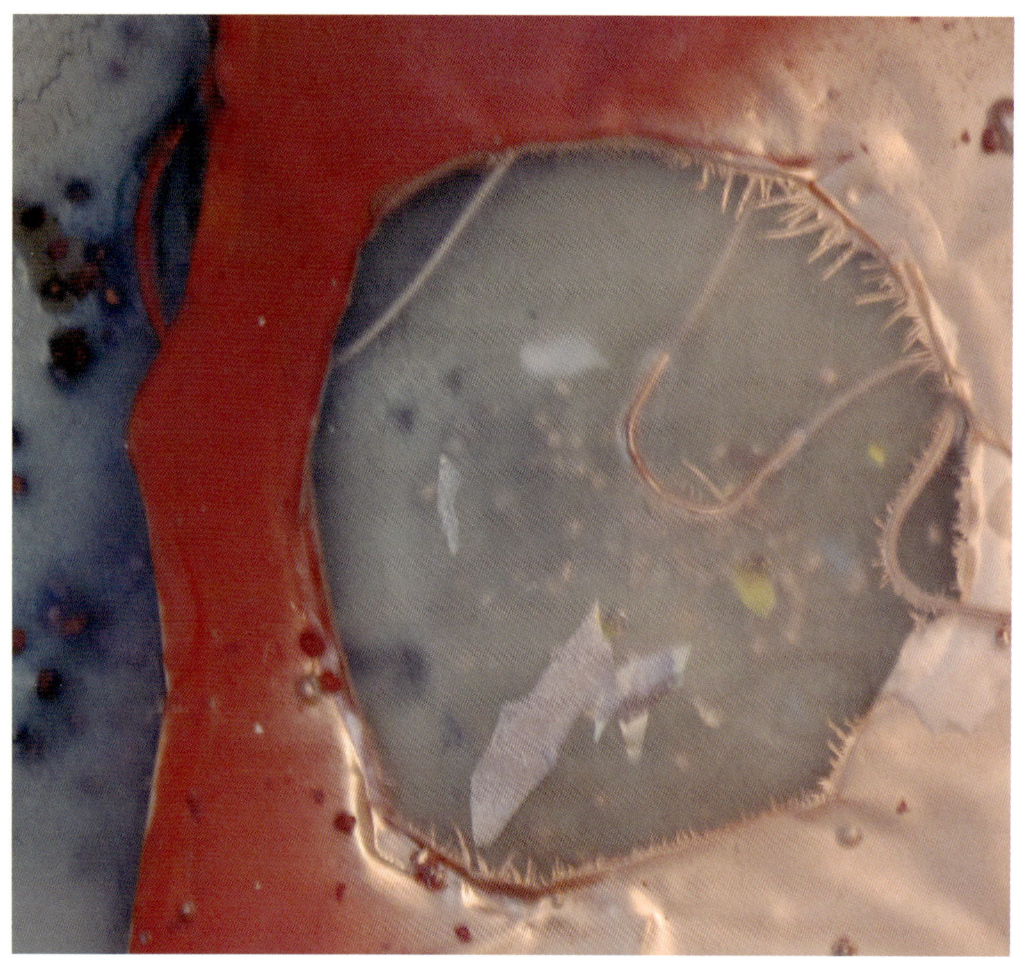

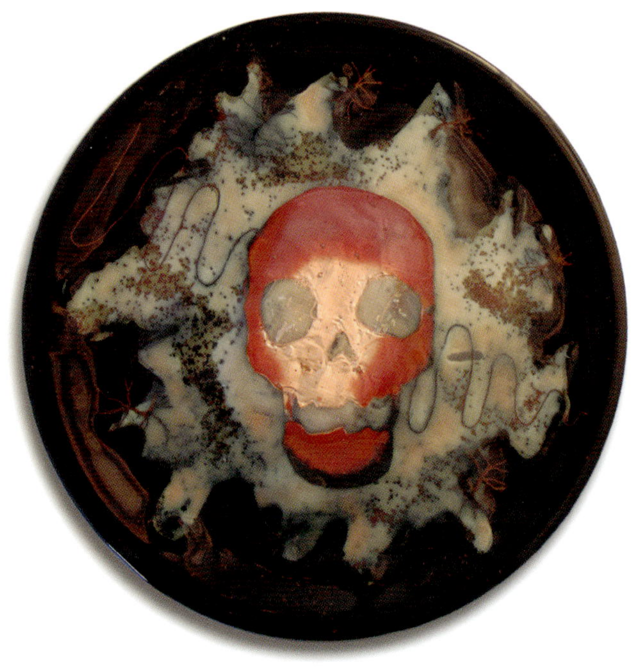

93. *12" X 12" Plate – Untitled - Part of Dana's 'black period'*

Understanding the 'bright spot' (unoxidized copper) Dana has placed the skull in the center of the plate taking advantage of the color variation for shading. During fusing, the initial slumping starts in the center, keeping the air from oxidizing the copper.

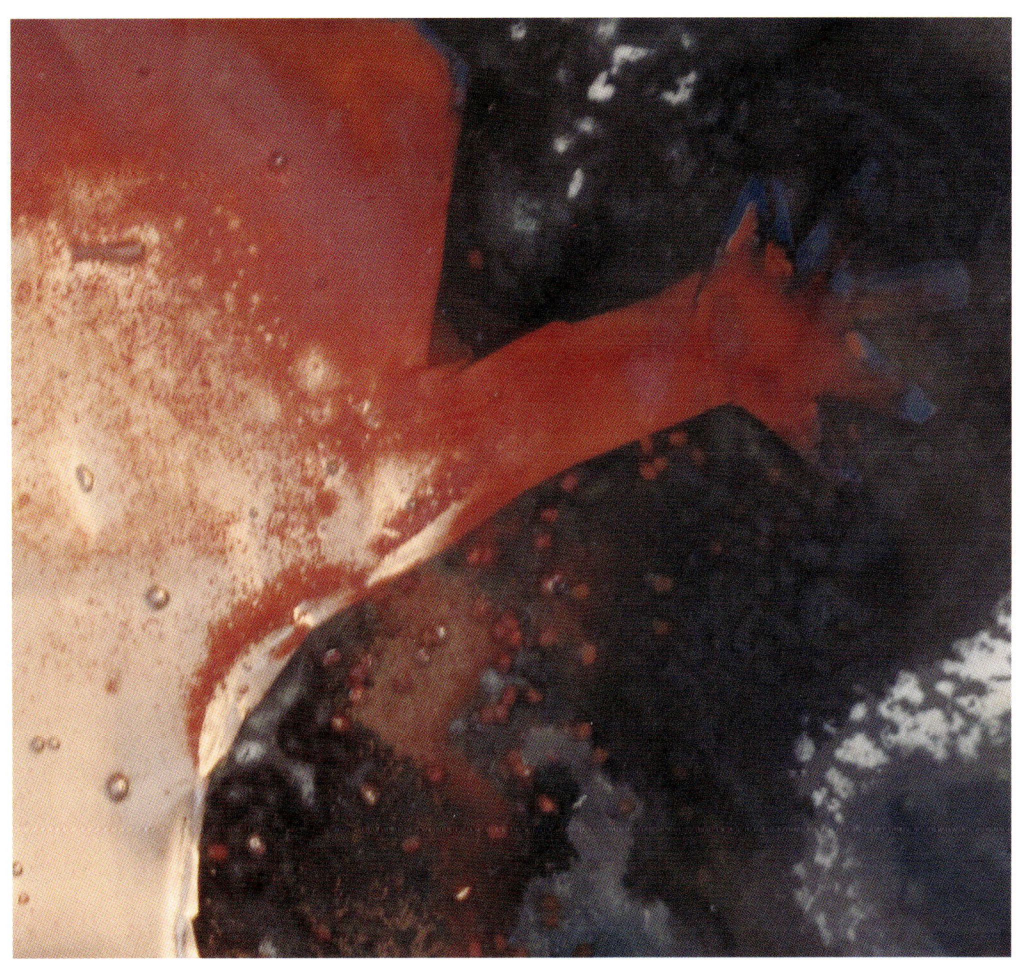

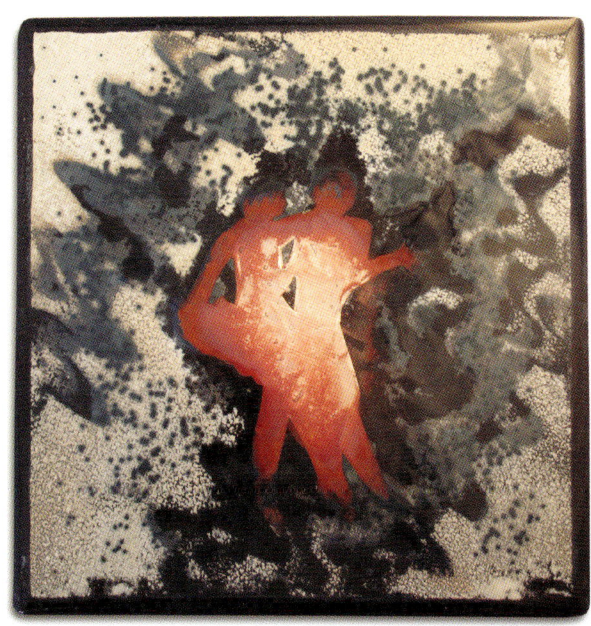

94. *Dancing In the Dark 10" X 10" tile.*

Sprayed dry enamel on background allowed to dry. Straight lines of dry fine copper were combed when Dana drew her finger across the dry blank, creating the wavy smeared pattern.

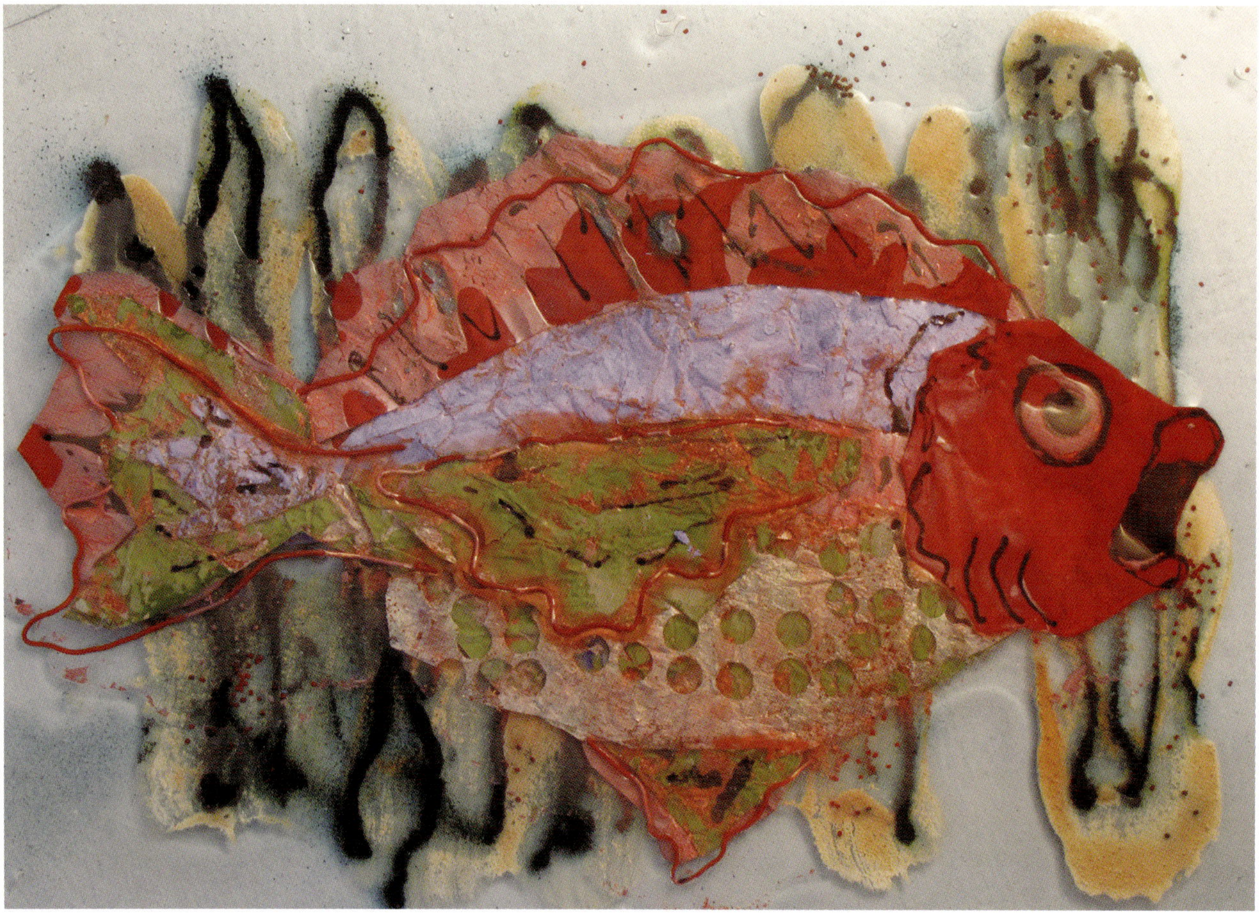

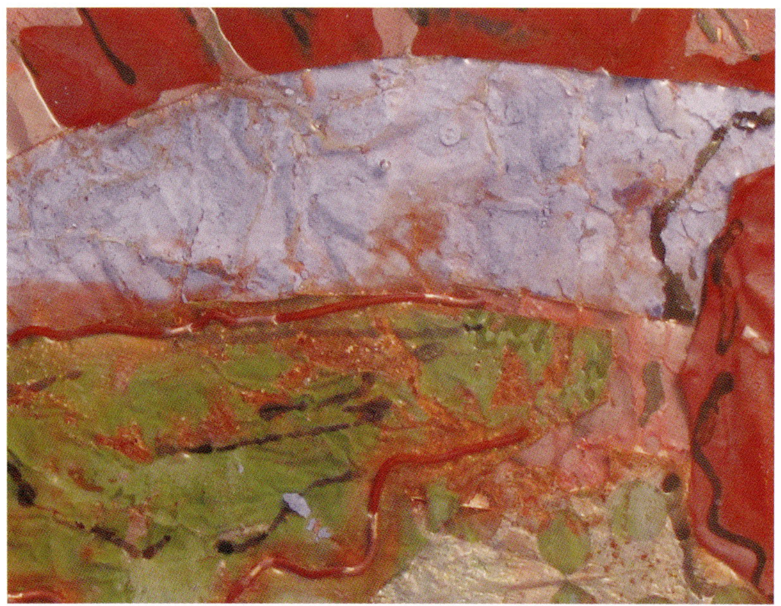

93. *"Five Pound Bass" by Dana Taylor, Enhanced*

Using painted aluminum foil overlaying copper fish with Glassline detail and dry fine copper seaweed. Copper wire outlines provide air escape passages. Close-up actual size.

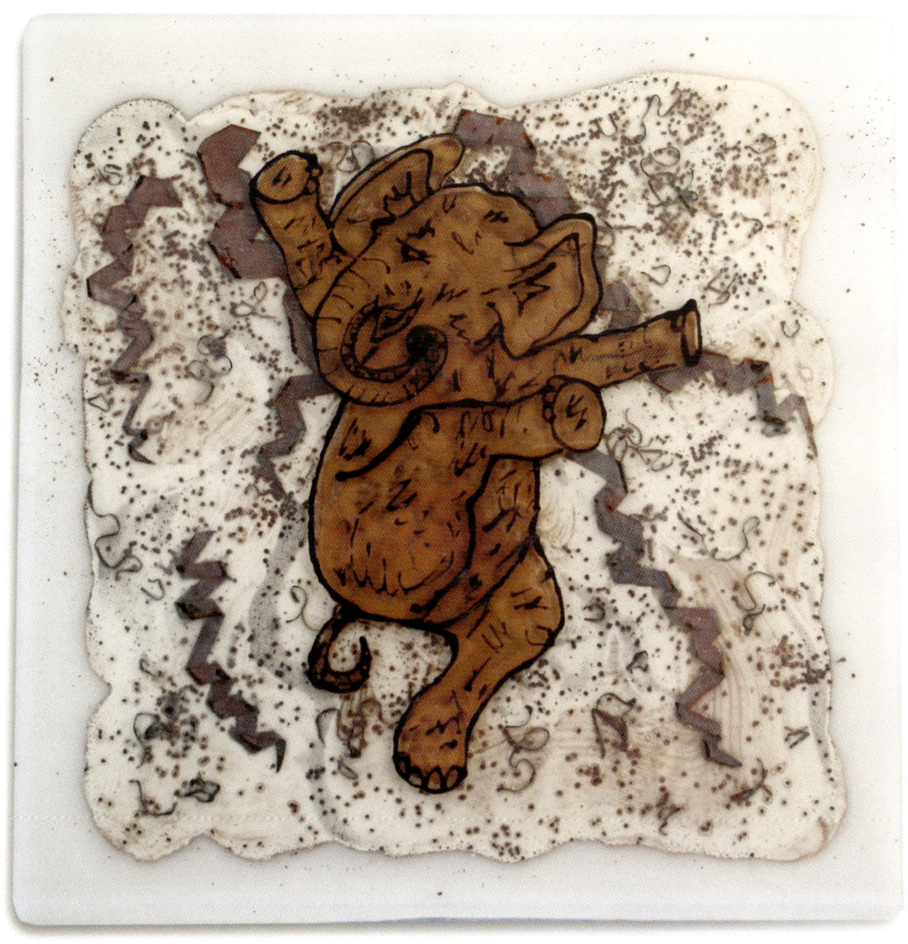

93. *"Party Time"*
Boyce's Comments: This elephant is the only Republican in the House. The Republicans are dancing in the street after taking over the House of Representatives.

Brown & Green Reactive Dry Enamel on the bottom white blank with confetti copper strips and granules. The elephant was outlined on the top of the clear blank, allowed to dry then turned over and painted with orange Glassline.

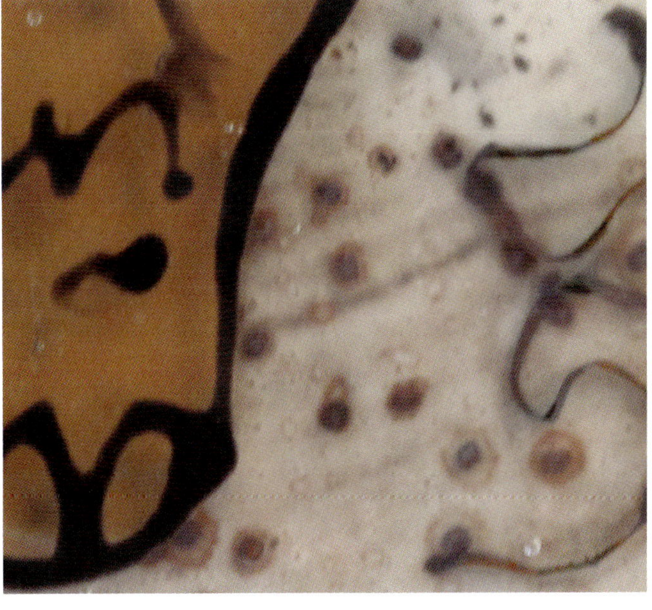

Recommended Suppliers

Axner Pottery Supply – www.axner.com

Go to Axner & find "Fusing Farm" also a great source for metal oxides & carbonates.

Boyce Lundstrom – www.Boycelundstrom.com

Source of supplies created by Boyce, not found other places.

CBS – Coating by Sandberg – www.cbs-dichroic.com

Dichroic coated copper foil. Makes dichro confetti.

Delphi – www.Delphiglass.com

Source of everything not found on www.boycelundstrom.com or www.michealdupille.com

Glassline – www.Clayartcenter.com

Many colors to add to glass in squirt bottles.

Harbor Freight – www.Harborfreight.com

Best source of craft tools in the United States

JenKen – www.JenKenKilns.com

Maker of fast fire fiber fuser, Yahoo Raku.

Laguna Clay Co. – www.Lagunaclay.com

Basic ceramic materials.

Michael Dupille – www.Michaeldupille.com

Best source of CMC, also known as liquid stringer, glass glue etc, etc.

Nimrod Hall Copper Foil Co. – www.Nimrodhall.com

The name says it all.

Skutt Kilns – www.Skutt.com

Located in Portland, Oregon, a nice place to live and build kilns.

Slumpy's – www.Slumpys.com

Has a few molds I like to use.

The Paul Wissmach Glass Co., Inc. – www.Wissmachglass.com

Best price on clear, black & white fusible glass.

Uroboros Glass – www.Uroboros.com

Great sourceof 90 COE fusible, great color palette.

Youghiogheny Glass – www.youghioghenyglass.com

Source for Easy Fuse float fit colors for fusing.

Index

My side yard Highway 101 in Oceanside California.
Winter storm 2010.

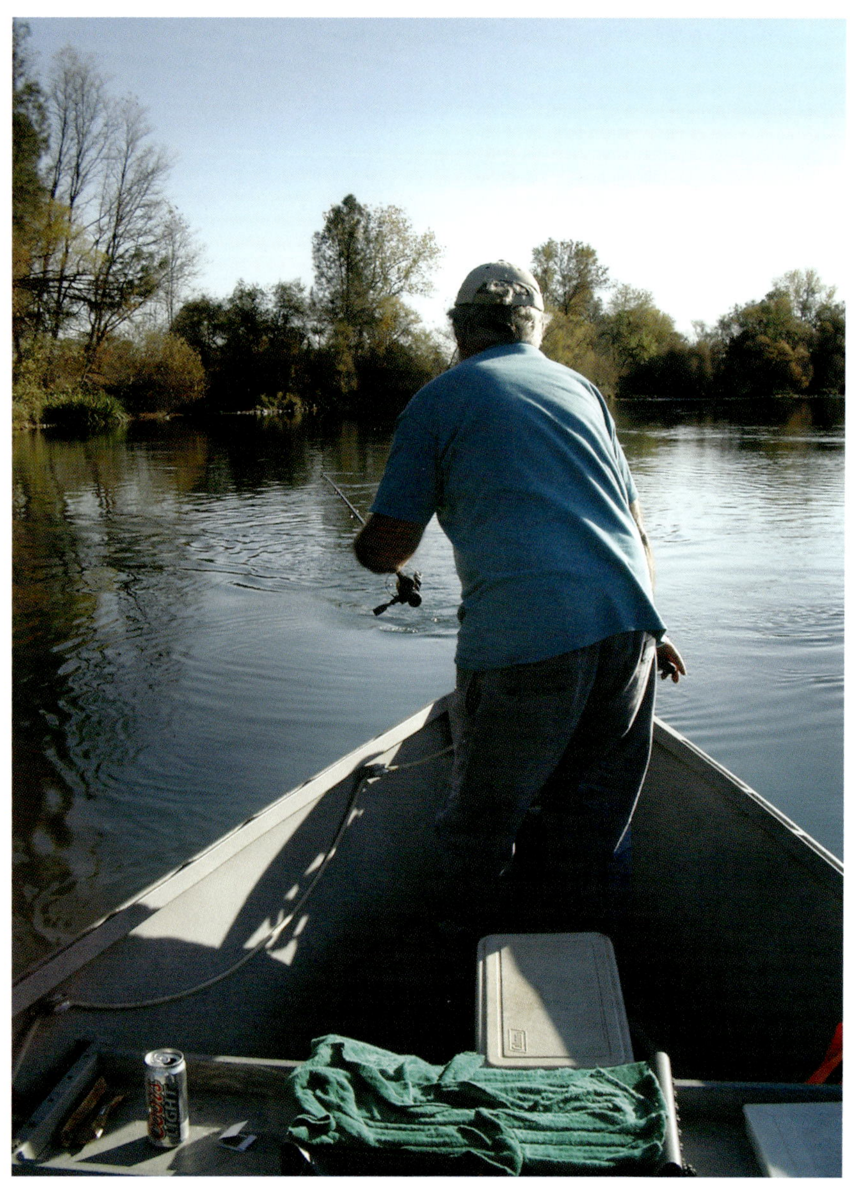

Clif's End